# The Art of
# Nonconversation

# The Art of
# Nonconversation

## A Reexamination of the
## Validity of the
## Oral Proficiency Interview

MARYSIA JOHNSON

Yale University Press    New Haven & London

PUBLISHER: Mary Jane Peluso
PRODUCTION CONTROLLER: Aldo Cupo
EDITORIAL ASSISTANT: Emily Saglimbeni
DESIGNER: James J. Johnson
Set in Stemple Garamond type by Integrated Publishing Solutions,
Grand Rapids, Michigan.
Printed in the United States of America by Victor Graphics,
Baltimore, Maryland.

*Library of Congress Cataloging-in-Publication Data*

Johnson, Marysia
The art of noncoversation : a reexamination of the validity of the oral
proficiency interview / Marysia Johnson.
p. cm.
Includes bibligraphical references and index.
ISBN 0-300-09002-1 (alk. paper)

1. Language and languages—Ability testing.   2. Oral communication—Ability
testing.   3. Communicative competence—Ability testing.   I. Title
P53.6 .J64 2001
418′ .0076—dc21     2001001629
A catalogue record for this book is available from the British Library.

The paper in this book meets the guidelines for permanence and durability of
the Committee on Production Guidelines for Book Longevity of the Council
on Library Resources.

10 9 8 7 6 5 4 3 2 1

*To my family*

# Contents

# *Acknowledgments*

I would like to thank my dissertation committee members at Georgetown University, Jeff Connor-Linton, Deborah Schiffrin, and Eduardo Cascallar for their knowledge, support, and guidance.

I am deeply grateful to Jean Turner and Fred Davidson for their invaluable suggestions and comments on my manuscript and for their generous mentoring, encouragement, and friendship.

I thank the following people, who reviewed my book proposal and an initial draft of my manuscript and offered their comments and suggestions: Elana Shohamy, Tel Aviv University; Andrea Tyler, Georgetown University; Jean Turner, Monterey Institute of International Studies; and Rebecca Oxford, Columbia University.

Finally, I would like to thank my parents for instilling in me respect for knowledge, for raising me in the belief that knowledge transcends time and space.

# Abbreviations

| | |
|---|---|
| ACTFL | American Council on the Teaching of Foreign Languages |
| CA | Conversational Analysis |
| CLA | Communicative Language Ability |
| DA | Discourse Analysis |
| DLI | Defense Language Institute |
| ETS | Educational Testing Service |
| FSI | Foreign Service Institute |
| FLPTB | Federal Language Proficiency Testing Board |
| ILR | Interagency Language Roundtable |
| ITA | International Teaching Assistant |
| L1 | First Language |
| L2 | Second Language |
| OPI | Oral Proficiency Interview |
| POLA | Practical Oral Language Ability |
| SLA | Second Language Acquisition |
| SD | Semantic Differential |
| SPEAK | Speaking Proficiency English Assessment Kit |
| TOEIC | Test of English for International Communication |
| TOEFL | Test of English as a Foreign Language |
| TSE | Test of Spoken English |
| ZPD | Zone of Proximal Development |

# The Art of
# **Non**conversation

# OVERVIEW OF THE BOOK

The purpose of this book is to provide answers to two fundamental questions. The first is a practical one, and it represents the main focus of the book: Is the Oral Proficiency Interview a valid instrument for assessing language speaking proficiency? The second is a theoretical one: What is speaking ability? (that is, speaking ability that exists independently of testing instruments).

Currently, an interview is a common way of assessing speaking ability in a second/foreign language in the United States and around the world. In particular, the Oral Proficiency Interview (OPI) is a very popular instrument for assessing second/foreign language speaking proficiency in such U.S. government institutions as the Foreign Language Institute and the Defense Language Institute. It is also used by nongovernmental institutions like the Educational Testing Service (ETS) and the American Council on the Teaching of Foreign Languages (ACTFL).

In the OPI, which is based on the ACTFL, the ETS, and the Interagency Language Roundtable (ILR) scale level descriptions, the examinee converses face-to-face with one or two trained testers on a variety of topics for ten to thirty minutes. The elicited sample is then rated on a scale ranging from 0 (no functional ability) to 5 (proficiency equivalent to that of a well-educated native speaker). Plus ratings are also assigned when the examinee's speaking proficiency exhibits features of the next higher level. Overall, the examinee's level of speaking proficiency is measured on an 11-point range scale.

It is estimated that several thousand OPIs are administered each year. Professional careers, future job assignments, pay increases, and entrance to or exit from college language programs frequently depend on the rating obtained in an OPI.

The question remains, however, whether the interview format represents the most appropriate and desirable method of assessing speaking ability in a second language. The proponents of the OPI claim that "a well-structured oral proficiency interview tests speaking ability in the real-life context—a conversation. It is almost by definition a valid measure of speaking ability" (ETS 1982: 13). However, one of the central characteristics of naturally occurring conversation—as Gumperz (1982), Sacks et al. (1974), and Wolfson (1976), among others, have pointed out—is that language users are largely unaware of how conversation is typically structured and managed. Much of everyday conversation is so deceptively familiar that people studying and testing language often overlook its fundamental characteristics. It is precisely on these grounds that van Lier (1989) has challenged the ETS's claim that it measures speaking ability in the context of a conversation. Van Lier (1984: 494) simply asks, "Is it really a conversation?"

The answer to the questions, What kind of speech event is the OPI? and Is it really a conversation? is fundamental to our understanding of the construct validity of the OPI. Construct validity is essential for making inferences about the individual's ability on the basis of his/her test score. Establishing construct validity is the focus of major debate and concern among testing experts at present.

Findings in discourse analysis (Schiffrin 1994) offer the testing community new and unique ways of investigating the construct validity of a test. That is, the application of various discourse techniques allows one to determine what it is that is measured by a test and not what is assumed or claimed to be measured. This methodology has been applied to the OPI data to determine the OPI's major discourse and linguistic features and to answer van Lier's question, "Is it really a conversation?"

Discourse analysis provides theoretical rationales for conducting empirical investigation, specifically, for gath-

ering empirical evidence as to the nature of the OPI communicative speech event. The empirical evidence in this book
is based on both quantitative and qualitative findings from
two studies: a discourse analysis study (chapter 5) and a semantic differential study of natives' perceptions of the OPI
communicative speech event (chapter 6). These combined
findings have led to the development of a prototypical model
of the OPI communicative speech event (chapter 7).

Chapters 8 and 9 investigate the issue, What is
speaking ability? (that is, speaking ability that exists independently of testing instruments). For that purpose, several
models of speaking ability are described and discussed: the
communicative competence models proposed by Hymes
(1972), Canale and Swain (1980), and Bachman (1990); the
interactional competence model (Young 1998, 1999); and a
model of spoken interaction based on Vygotsky's sociocultural theory.

Although Vygotsky's sociocultural theory is a theory of learning and not performance, its foci on social interaction and on the individual's potential development
offer a challenge to current thinking about testing speaking
ability. That is, Vygotsky's emphasis on social interaction
represents a direct challenge to the current testing view of
interaction as cognitive and psycholinguistic. Hence, if a
Vygotskian framework were integrated with the OPI, the
shift of attention from the individual's current development to his/her potential development would require some

revisions of the existing rating scales and of subcomponents included in various rating scales.

In sum, the book deals with the issue of the construct validity of the OPI. The book presents some practical information as to the ways discourse analysis techniques can be utilized in determining construct validity. The OPI's validity is investigated within the framework of Messick's (1989: 13) definition of validity, which is viewed as "an integrated evaluative judgment of the degree to which empirical evidence and theoretical rationales support the adequacy and appropriateness of inferences and actions based on test scores."

The book also proposes a new model of language ability—the Practical Oral Language Ability (POLA) based on Vygotsky's sociocultural theory that considers language ability to be reflective of sociocultural and institutional contexts in which the language has been acquired.

# Chapter 2

# THE GENESIS AND
# EVOLUTION OF THE
# OPI SYSTEM

The history of the Oral Proficiency Interview, as presented in Lowe 1983, 1986, Clark and Clifford 1988, and Valdman 1988, is closely associated with the efforts of the Foreign Service Institute (FSI) of the U.S. Department of State in the early 1950s to develop proficiency-based testing to evaluate the foreign functional language skills of its employees. Dissatisfied with the existing language tests and procedures based on multiple choice and other discrete-item approaches, the FSI developed a series of verbally defined levels of general speaking proficiency. These descriptions were based on a needs analysis that was conducted to identify typical language use requirements of the FSI graduates in various foreign language posts. The resulting scale consisted of five levels, ranging from basic survival competency (Level 1—Elementary Proficiency) up to the native competency of an educated native speaker of the language (Level 5—Native or Bilingual Proficiency).

By 1956, OPI testing had become mandatory for all foreign service officers. A year later the OPI testing system was adopted by a number of other governmental agencies, including the Defense Language Institute (DLI), the Central Intelligence Agency (CIA), the Federal Bureau of Investigation (FBI), and the Peace Corps, to assess the foreign language speaking capabilities of U.S. government and military employees (Lowe 1983).

The governmental agencies' unified efforts to modify and refine the FSI system led to the development of the Interagency Language Roundtable (ILR) skill level descriptions and eventually to the extension of the original FSI scale to include the plus levels. In the process, the FSI 5-point scale became an 11-point scale.

The Peace Corps played a crucial role in introducing the FSI proficiency scale and interview to nongovernmental institutions. In the late 1960s, the Peace Corps called on the Educational Testing Service (ETS) to assist in developing a training and interviewing program to test the oral proficiency of its volunteers in various training sites worldwide. Prior to their travel to locations to teach Peace Corps staff how to use the OPI techniques, the ETS staff members themselves became familiar with the FSI scale and interviewing procedures. Thus, for the first time, the FSI oral proficiency testing system became known to the nongovernmental community.

The success and visibility of the ETS/Peace Corps joint project contributed to a rapidly growing interest in the FSI testing system outside traditional governmental institutions. In response to this interest, the FSI, under Dean of Foreign Languages James Firth conducted a series of OPI familiarization workshops for various academic institutions in the late 1970s and early 1980s.

Interest in the OPI system was further heightened when ETS, and later the American Council on the Teaching of Foreign Languages (ACTFL), received a grant from the U.S. Department of Education to develop a set of proficiency definitions for universities, high schools, elementary schools, and businesses under the name of the Common Metric project.

ACTFL modified the ILR scale to give it finer increments at the lower end of the proficiency scale. The ACTFL scale includes more gradations between the ILR levels 0+ and 2. Table 2.1 presents the ACTFL/ETS and ILR scale values (Lowe 1983).

Because of their similarities, the ACTFL/ETS and ILR scales have been jointly referred to as the AEI scale, the acronym created from the first letters of the scales (Lowe 1986). This acronym, however, has not been widely accepted. The OPI testing community tends to maintain a

| ACTFL/ETS | ILR |
|---|---|
| Superior | 3 and higher, i.e., 3+ 4 4+ 5 |
| Advanced Plus | 2+ |
| Advanced | 2 |
| Intermediate High | 1+ |
| Intermediate Mid | 1 |
| Intermediate Low | 1 |
| Novice High | 0+ |
| Novice Mid | 0 |
| Novice Low | 0 |

Table 2.1   ACTFL/ETS/ILR Scales

sense of separateness among the scales, although the similarities among these three scales are clearly visible. This can be illustrated by the following definitions of the ILR level 2 and the ACTFL Advanced Level:

*ILR Level 2*
Able to satisfy routine social demands and limited work requirements. Can handle with confidence but not with facility most normal, high frequency social situations including extensive but casual conversations about current events, as well as work, family, and autobiographical information. (Lowe 1988: Appendix V-3)

*ACTFL Advanced Level*
Able to satisfy the requirements of everyday situations and routine school and work requirements. Can handle with confidence, but not with facility, complicated tasks and social situations, such as elaborating, complaining, and apologizing. Can narrate and describe

with some details. Can communicate facts and talk casually about topics of current public and personal interest, using general vocabulary. (American Council on the Teaching of Foreign Languages 1986: 2)

In the early 1980s, the OPI underwent major internal changes with respect to both the elicitation procedures involved in a well-conducted interview and the rating procedures. The efforts of Lowe and Clifford at the CIA led to the establishment of tester training workshops and such tester training materials as the *ILR Handbook on Oral Interview Testing.*

Higgs and Clifford (1982) introduced the functional trisection to the OPI system. The *functional trisection* had major conceptual implications for both elicitation and ratings procedures. The functional trisection includes three components: "*Function* that refers to the types of language use task that the speaker is expected to be able to carry out at the specified level; *content* that refers to the kinds of topics or subject areas at issue in the communication, and *accuracy* that describes the degree of structural, lexical, and phonological precision with which the examinee is able to communicate" (Clark and Clifford 1988: 38).

In 1992, on the initiative of the U.S. Congress, the Federal Language Proficiency Testing Board (FLPTB) was created at the Center for the Advancement of Language Learning in Washington, D.C. The FLPTB effort concentrated primarily on improving and refining the OPI used for assessing general speaking proficiency across all governmental agencies (that is, the development of new elicitation techniques, tester training program, and rating procedures). The FLPTB, however, was dissolved a couple of years later after having implemented some changes to the OPI tester training program within such governmental agencies as the Defense Language Institute in Monterey, California.

## The OPI's Structure, Elicitation Techniques, and Rating Procedures

### Structure of the OPI

The OPI has both a general and a level-specific structure as described in the *ILR Handbook on Oral Interview Testing* Lowe (1988), and in Clark and Clifford (1988). The OPI consists of four phases: warm-up, level check, probes, and wind-down.

The *warm-up* phase consists of social amenities at a level that is designed to be very easy for the candidate. There are three purposes for the warm-up: (1) putting the candidate at ease; (2) reacquainting the candidate with the language (if necessary); and (3) giving the testers a preliminary indication of the candidate's level. This preliminary indication must be confirmed in the next phase of the interview, the level check.

The purpose of the *level check* is to determine the candidate's highest sustainable level of speaking proficiency. In the level check phase, testers have the candidate perform the tasks assigned to a given level. When the candidate successfully passes the level check, his/her performance provides a floor for the rating. The next phase, probes, aims at finding the ceiling.

The purpose of the *probes* phase is to show the tester(s) whether the candidate has reached his/her highest level of speaking proficiency. To probe, testers have the candidate attempt to perform a task or tasks one level above the level of level check. The level check and probes are interwoven, so that the candidate is being alternately stressed and relaxed, not constantly pushed ever higher.

The last phase of the general structure of the interview is called the *wind-down*. The purpose of this phase is to leave the candidate with a feeling of accomplishment. It also gives testers a last chance to check any aspect of the candidate's speaking ability that may be incompletely assessed.

## The OPI Elicitation Techniques

To obtain a ratable sample, that is, a sample to which a rating can be assigned, testers must make sure that level-specific requirements as well as general requirements have been fulfilled. Level-specific requirements include a series of tasks and functions that are assigned to a given level. To elicit level-specific tasks and functions, testers use questions and role-play situations as the main elicitation techniques.

A variety of question types constitute the core of the OPI elicitation procedures. A given set of question types is recommended for a particular level or levels of speaking proficiency. Thus, for level 0+, yes/no and choice questions are required; for levels 1 and 2, information questions; for levels 3, 4, and 5, hypothetical and supported opinion questions. The following are examples of the question types (Lowe 1988):

> Yes/no:
>> Do you live in Washington?
> Choice:
>> Would you like tea or coffee?
> Information:
>> What did you do last summer?
> Hypothetical:
>> If you were the prime minister, what would you do to improve the economic situation in your country?
> Supported opinion:
>> Why are you against this type of policy?

In addition to the types of questions indicated above, the OPI elicitation techniques may include role-play situations. At the higher levels (levels 3, 4, and 5), the testers are encouraged to use several role-play situations to elicit the required tasks, such as convincing, advising, persuading, and so on. Thus a sample OPI for the candidate who is at level 3+ or 4 may include more role-play situations than for one at level 2 or 1+.

## Principles of the OPI Rating Procedures

In the OPI, the ratings are expressed in global terms. The totality of the candidate's speaking performance is compared to the ILR descriptions at each level. There are six factors that contribute to the candidate's overall speaking proficiency: pronunciation, fluency, grammar, vocabulary, and sociolinguistic/cultural factor. The candidate's level of speaking proficiency is evaluated to reflect his/her ability to integrate all these factors/skills in performing a variety of language functions. The OPI is thus an integrative test (Lowe 1983, 1986, 1988).

## The OPI's General Test Characteristics

In 1983, Lowe claimed that six major features of the OPI distinguished it from other types of speaking tests administered in U.S. schools and colleges up to the early 1980s:

1. The OPI is a proficiency test, i.e., it tests a candidate's speaking ability as compared to a language as it is spoken by well-educated native speakers.

2. The test stresses the functional, foreign language real-life situations in which the language is employed.
3. The test maintains content validity by including in the interview questions that test language functions and real-life situations.
4. The OPI is an integrative, not a discrete-point test.
5. The OPI scale is noncompensatory at the upper end, that is, as of level 3 the candidate cannot compensate for weakness in one subskill by using a strength in another; a stronger grammar, for instance, cannot compensate for a weaker vocabulary.
6. The OPI assigns a global rating. One rating expresses the candidate's overall speaking ability. (Lowe 1983: 233–35)

## The OPI's Reliability and Validity

Throughout the OPI's history, in addition to the above-mentioned characteristics, the OPI's reliability (Adams 1978; Clark 1986; Magnan 1987; Dandonolli and Henning 1990; Stansfield and Kenyon 1992; Thompson 1995) and validity (Clark 1978, 1980, 1986; Lowe 1983, 1986; Clark and Clifford 1988) have been often pointed out to illustrate its superiority over other tests of speaking ability.

Traditionally, *reliability* refers to the consistency of measurement from one occasion to another, from one test to another. In objectively scored tests such as multiple choice tests, reliability is usually estimated by internal consistency, which determines how well the items on a test correlate with each other. In subjectively scored tests, such as essays or the OPI, two methods are applied: inter-rater reliability and intra-rater reliability. Inter-rater reliability determines how closely two or more testers agree in their judgments of the individual's performance. Intra-rater reliability establishes how closely the tester agrees with himself/ herself in assessing the same individual's performance on two different occasions.

The reliability of the ILR Oral Proficiency Interview is considered to be higher than the reliability of the ACTFL Oral Proficiency Interview. For example, Adams (1978) studied the reliability of the OPI in German and French at the FSI and found it to be .91. Clark (1986) conducted the reliability study between French and German testers from two institutions, the DLI and the CIA, and found it to be rather close. Stansfield and Kenyon (1992) used Clark's data to calculate test-retest reliability and found it to be .92, which is considered to be very high for a speaking test.

The ACTFL reliability is slightly lower than the ILR reliability (usually within .80 range). Thompson (1995) attributes this to the fact that most of the ACTFL testers are scattered around the country and thus do not have a chance to discuss their ratings with other testers. The ACTFL testers also have fewer opportunities to attend recertification and refresher workshops.

The *validity* of the OPI is primarily viewed in the traditional, pre-Messick (1989) types of validity terms. In the next chapter, I shall explain in detail the traditional, pre-Messick, and post-Messick views of validity. Here, however, I shall describe the OPI's validity as seen by its proponents in terms of three types: face validity, content validity, and predictive validity.

*Face validity* concerns the extent to which a test *looks as if* it measures what it is supposed to measure (Hughes 1989). For instance, according to the proponents of the system, the fact that the OPI has the format of a face-to-face interaction, and not a multiple choice format, alone improves substantially the face validity and overall validity of the OPI test.

Traditionally, *content validity* refers to the extent to which the content of the test includes representative samples of the domain to be measured. If one is to judge whether or not a test has content validity, test specifications need to be compared against test content (Hughes 1989; Bachman 1990; Davidson and Lynch forthcoming). The OPI claims to maintain content validity by "including in each interview questions that test language functions and real-life situations" (Lowe 1983: 235).

Clark (1978b: 23) also claims that the content validity of direct tests like the OPI should be "evaluated by informal inspection rather than through statistical means." He identifies the most important feature of direct tests:

The informal correspondence between the setting and operation of the testing procedure and the setting and operation of the real-life situation constitutes the face/content validity of the test—the basic psychometric touchstone for direct proficiency (Clark 1978b: 23).

*Predictive validity* concerns the degree to which a test can predict the individual's future performance (Hughes 1989). As a justification for the implementation of the OPI system in academia, Lowe (1986) points to the OPI's high predictive validity. He claims that the OPI has been used successfully by the government for more than thirty years, thus implying high predictive value of the test relative to candidates' real-life performance.

## The OPI and the Proficiency Movement

The proponents of the OPI system—Lowe (1983, 1986, 1988), Clark (1978b, 1980, 1986), Clark and Clifford (1988), Clark and Lett (1988), Higgs and Clifford (1982), Omaggio (1986), and Liskin-Gasparro (1984)—have made attempts to popularize the ACTFL OPI by applying it to teaching, curricula, and evaluation of foreign language proficiency at universities and colleges. The efforts to promulgate the OPI within academia initiated the movement that has come to be known as the proficiency movement.

The *proficiency movement* tries to establish the model of language proficiency manifested in the ACTFL/

ETS/ILR documents as the theoretical model for teaching and assigning communicative language ability. In the context of the OPI, proficiency has been defined as the "ability to use language for real-life purpose" (Clark 1972: 5). In the opinion of the proponents of the OPI system, the real-life performance as well as the face-to-face format constitute the ultimate reason for the system to be fully implemented in a variety of contexts such as government, academia, and business and to treat it as the main instrument for assessing second and foreign language speaking proficiency.

# Cha 3 pter

# A CRITICAL APPRAISAL
# OF THE OPI

A large group of researchers working in the fields of language testing and teaching has voiced strong criticism of the ACTFL / ETS / ILR. Bachman (1988, 1990), Bachman and Savignon (1986), Lantolf and Frawley (1985, 1988) also warned against institutionalization of the OPI prior to conducting a thorough empirical investigation of the OPI system and prior to establishing the sound theory of proficiency, on which the OPI is claimed to be based. The institutionalization of the OPI, however, is evident not only in the context of government and academia, but in the business community as well.

In the early 1990s, the Test of English for International Communication (TOEIC) Language Proficiency Interview (LPI) was developed on the basis of the FSI/ILR scale description. TOEIC LPI is now used worldwide to measure English proficiency in the workplace other than academia. To illustrate how closely the TOEIC adheres to the FSI/ILR scale, let's compare the ILR level 3 with the TOEIC level 3:

> *TOEIC LPI Level Description:*
> *Level 3 (General Professional Proficiency)*
> *Able to speak the language with sufficient structural accuracy and vocabulary to participate effectively in most formal and informal conversations on practical, social, and professional topics.*
> Nevertheless, the individual's limitations generally restrict the professional contexts of language use to matters of shared knowledge and/or international convention. Discourse is cohesive. The individual uses the language acceptably, but with some noticeable imperfections; yet, errors virtually never interfere with understanding and rarely disturb the native speaker. (TOEIC Language Proficiency Interview Manual 1996: 63)

> *ILR Skill Level Description*
> *Level 3 (General Professional Proficiency)*
> *Able to speak the language with sufficient structural accuracy and vocabulary to participate effectively in most formal and informal conversations on practical, social, and professional topics.*
> Nevertheless, the individual's limitations generally restrict the professional contexts of language use to matters of shared knowledge and/or international convention. Discourse is cohesive. The individual uses

the language acceptably, but with some noticeable imperfections; yet, errors virtually never interfere with understanding and rarely disturb the native speaker. (Lowe 1988: Appendix V-4)

From these examples, it is evident that the warning against institutionalization of the OPI prior to conducting a thorough empirical investigation of the OPI system has had little impact on the popularization of the OPI system within second and foreign language communities. With the establishment of the TOEIC as the worldwide standard for measuring English proficiency within the business community, we have entered an era of a total monopolization of the OPI system within academia, government, and business.

In addition, the popularity of the OPI system is reinforced by the power of the institutions that develop and administer it, including the Foreign Service Institute, the Defense Language Institute, and the Educational Testing Service. This could be perceived as an attempt to "communize," or totally control, foreign/second language testing worldwide through one system that is promoted by two or three powerful language testing institutions.

Under such circumstances, it is even more vital to address the issue of the OPI's validity. Current and future users of the system must be able to make an informed decision as to "the adequacy and appropriateness of inferences and actions based on test scores" (Messick 1989: 13).

# A Historical Overview of the Definition of Validity

The term *validity* has undergone major conceptual changes over the past years. Because the premise of this book is to investigate the validity of the OPI to determine what it is that the OPI measures, I shall briefly review the history of validation in language testing. The goal of this review is to familiarize the reader with past and current definitions of validity. Readers are encouraged to refer to the works of Messick 1989, Bachman 1990, Moss 1992, and Chapelle 1994, 1999 for in-depth analyses of the genesis and evolution of validation in language testing and educational measurement.

The definition of validity is important for all test users because "accepted practices of the validation are critical to decisions about what constitutes a good language test for a particular situation" (Chapelle 1999: 254). Despite an ongoing debate on how exactly validation should be defined and executed, one can identify two major periods in the history of validation in language testing marked by the publication of Messick's 1989 seminal work *Validity*. These two periods can be labeled the pre-Messick and the post-Messick.

The pre-Messick, traditional definition of validity is primarily associated with different *types* of validity, such as content validity, predictive validity, concurrent validity, and construct validity. The three traditional type-focused definitions of face, content, and predictive validity were addressed in chapter 2. Here I shall define *concurrent* and *construct validity.*

*Concurrent validity* is established when the test and a criterion measure are administered at about the same time, and the student's scores on the test are compared with his/her test scores on the other instrument that serves as a criterion (Hughes 1989; Bachman 1990).

*Construct validity* refers to the underlying theory of a test (Hughes 1989), and it "concerns the extent to which performance on tests is consistent with predications that we make on the basis of a theory of abilities, or construct" (Bachman 1988: 51).

Messick 1989 proposed a new definition: "Validity is an integrated evaluative judgment of the degree to which empirical evidence and theoretical rationales support the *adequacy* and *appropriateness* of *inferences* and *actions* based on test scores" (Messick 1989: 3). The key points of Messick's 1989 definition of validity can be summarized as follows: First, validity is seen as a unified but multifaceted concept. As a unified (that is, integrated) evaluative judgment, Messick's definition of validity undermines the traditional view of validity represented by different types of validity. Second, according to Messick, validation is a scientific endeavor and requires theoretical and empirical investigations. Third, validity is "a matter of degree, not all or none" (Messick 1989: 13). Fourth, validity is a property of test scores, not of tests. Prior to Messick, validity was portrayed as an all-or-nothing characteristic of a language test and not as a property of test scores. For example, Lado (1961: 321) defines validity as follows: "Does a test measure what it is supposed to measure? If it does, it is valid." Messick rejects this assumption. Messick (1989: 14) states, "Tests do not have reliabilities and validities, only test responses do. This is an important point because test responses are a function not only of the items, tasks, and stimulus conditions, but of the *persons* responding and the *context* of measurement." Fifth, Messick stresses the social consequences of test interpretation and uses, for example, social actions based on test scores.

For Messick, *construct validity* is an overarching validity concept. The centrality and importance of construct validity is evident in Messick's "progressive matrix." This progressive matrix is constructed out of two interconnected facets of the unitary validity concept. One facet pertains to the outcome of the testing (test interpretation and test use), while the other refers to the types of arguments or justifications (the evidential basis and the consequential basis) that should be used to justify the outcome of the testing (Messick 1989).

According to Messick, in order to justify a particular interpretation of test scores, we must gather evidence (that is, present arguments) for construct validity and consider the social consequences of such an interpretation. The matrix is progressive because each of the four cells includes construct validity but adds additional features (table 3.1).

Messick 1989 identifies several distinct types of evidence that can be used in the validation process:

> We can look at the content of a test in relation to the content of the domain of reference. We can probe the ways in which individuals respond to item or task. We can examine relationships among responses to the tasks, items, or parts of the test, that is, the internal structure of test responses. We can survey relationships of the test scores with other measures and background variables, that is the test's external structure. We can investigate differences in these test processes and structures over time, across groups and settings, and in response to experimental interventions, such as instructional or therapeutic treatment and manipulation of content, task requirements, or motivational conditions. Finally, we can trace the social consequences of interpreting and using the test scores in particular ways, scrutinizing not only the intended outcomes but also the unintended side effects. (Messick 1989: 16)

Some examples of validity evidence or arguments enumerated in the above quote, such as content and criterion validity, are similar to traditional types of validity. Messick's final type of evidence, the social consequences of "using

| Source of | Outcome of Testing | |
| Arguments | *Test Interpretation* | *Test Use* |
| --- | --- | --- |
| **Evidential Basis** | Construct validity | Construct validity<br>+ Relevance/Utility |
| **Consequential Basis** | Construct validity<br>+ Value implications | Construct validity<br>+ Relevance/Utility<br>+ Value implications<br>+ Social consequences |

Table 3.1   Facets of Validity
(after Messick 1989 and Bachman 1990)

the test scores in particular ways," represents an addition to the notion of validity.

Messick's 1989 definition of validity was introduced to the language teaching and testing community primarily through the work of Bachman 1990, who also defines validity as a unitary concept for test interpretation and use and views construct validity as an overarching concept.

The major differences between past and current conceptions of validity can be summarized as follows (Messick 1989; Bachman 1990; Chapelle 1999):

1. Currently, validity is considered a unitary concept with construct validity as an overarching/central concept. Validity is seen as a process of collecting evidence or arguments for a particular test score in-

terpretation and use. The process of validation can be viewed as "building a case" for or against a particular test score interpretation and its uses. In contrast, validity in the past was investigated in terms of types, with construct validity seen as one type of validity. Validity in the traditional, pre-Messick period was frequently determined through correlation procedures.

2. In the traditional, pre-Messick's view of validity, reliability, or consistency of measurement, was considered to be one of two important qualities of language testing. In fact, reliability was seen as a prerequisite for validity: in order for the test to be valid, it had to be reliable first. Within the current, post-Messick view of validity, reliability can be used as one of the arguments, that is, types of evidence, for validity (Chapelle 1994, 1999).

## A Critical Analysis of the OPI

As mentioned earlier, a large group of researchers working in the fields of language testing and teaching has voiced strong criticism of the ACTFL/ETS/ILR OPI. The most notable critics of the OPI system—Bachman (1988, 1990), Bachman and Savignon (1986), Lantolf and Frawley (1985, 1988), Savignon (1985)—focus their criticism of the OPI on the following:

1. the OPI's validity;
2. the ACTFL/ETS/ILR scale;

3. the OPI's rating procedures;
4. the OPI's native speaker norm;
5. the OPI's theory of proficiency.

Bachman (1988: 149) claims that "the validity of the ACTFL Oral Proficiency Interview as it is currently designed and used cannot be adequately examined, much less demonstrated, because it confounds abilities with elicitation procedures in its design, and it provides only a single rating, which has no basis in either theory or research." In this statement, Bachman raises two major issues: the OPI's validity, especially its construct validity, and its rating procedures.

The OPI's construct validity is impossible to demonstrate because the interpretation of candidates' scores beyond the testing context is severely hindered. Bachman (1988, 1990) attributes this to the test design itself, which is based on the functional trisection. The functional trisection does not allow one to make a distinction between the ability to be measured and the features of the context in which language performance takes place. To illustrate this point, let us take the ILR level 2 as an example. In the definition of level 2, references are made to specific language use contexts, specific topics, and specific functions:

*Level 2:*
*Context:* everyday situations, work, family etc.

*Content:* concrete topics such as own background, work, travel etc.

*Function:* narrate, describe, give directions and instructions, etc.

(Lowe 1983: 234)

As indicated above, the ability to be measured is strongly connected with the described context, content, and function. Extrapolating an individual's performance beyond these contexts is limited, which is to say, the generalizability of the scores to other contexts is restricted. Thus according to Bachman, the claim that the OPI appropriately measures real-life proficiency is misleading, and the users of the system, including test-takers, should be clearly informed about the limitations of the interpretability of the OPI scores beyond its context.

In Bachman's opinion, the OPI's content validity—the type of validity most frequently evoked by the OPI's proponents in their support of the test's validity—also cannot be determined or even properly investigated because the domain from which the content of the test is sampled is not precisely defined. The notion of real life as a domain is too vast and too subjective. The claim that the OPI maintains its content validity by including in each interview questions that test real-life situations is undermined by the fact that the basic requirement for establishing content validity (that is, that the domain to be measured be well defined) is not satisfied.

Bachman (1990), quoting a prominent psychometrist, Cronbach (1984), also discredits confidence in the OPI's face validity as the basis for demonstrating its validity:

> A test that seems relevant to the lay person is said to have "face validity." Adopting a test just because it appears reasonable is bad practice; many a "good-looking" test has had poor validity. Such evidence as this (reinforced by the whole history of phrenology, graphology, and tests of witchcraft!) warns against adopting a test solely because it is plausible. Validity of interpretation should not be compromised for the sake of face validity. (Cronbach 1984: 182–83, cited in Bachman 1990: 286)

Bachman further objects to the OPI rating procedure, and in particular to its one global rating. He claims that evidence from numerous language testing research studies consistently indicates that language proficiency consists of several distinct abilities. The global approach to rating proficiency reflects the obsolete theory of Oller's (1979) unitary trait hypothesis (which Oller subsequently rejected), according to which language proficiency consists of a single global ability. Ironically it seems that the OPI indirectly subscribes to the componential view of language ability by including in its design and rating procedures a functional trisection composed of three components: *function, content,* and *accuracy* (Bachman 1988, 1990); however, none of these three components is rated separately. Providing one global rating seems to erase the notion of the multicomponential nature of language ability.

Lantolf and Frawley (1985, 1988) share Bachman's skepticism about the claim that the OPI measures real-life proficiency. They dispute Liskin-Gasparro's (1984: 482) description of the OPI as a proficiency test that "measures, by definition, real-life proficiency." Lantolf and Frawley (1985) maintain that anything can be measured by definition. They assert that the ACTFL *Guidelines* artificially and experientially create a "real world" rather than empirically reflect it: "The *Guidelines* model reality; they do not mirror it. If the *Guidelines* measure reality by definition, they have construed a reality and therefore are the prescriptions of a theorist deciding what speakers ought to do" (Lantolf and Frawley 1985: 342).

Lantolf and Frawley (1985, 1988) consider the ACTFL *Guidelines* to be the product of theorists who have designed the levels of speaking proficiency by grading linguistic criteria into a taxonomy of difficulty levels that do not have any empirical foundation. To demonstrate this, they question Higgs and Clifford's assertion that the task of resolution of problem (level 3 task) is somehow less advanced than the task of persuasion (level 4 task).

Lantolf and Frawley (1985, 1988) also question the ultimate criterion of the so-called native speaker against which candidates' speaking language proficiency is compared. Along with Bachman (1990), they claim that the native speaker simply does not exist—only types of native speakers exist. The native speaker criterion also has a significant impact on the view of the OPI as a criterion-referenced test. Popham (1981: 28) states, "A criterion-referenced test is used to ascertain an individual's status with respect to a well-defined behavioral domain," while a norm-referenced test "is used to ascertain an individual's status with respect to the performance of other individuals on that test." The OPI is in reality a "hidden" norm-referenced test due to the fact that the candidate's performance is compared to that of "other individuals"—educated native speakers (Lantolf and Frawley 1985).

Lantolf and Frawley (1985) likewise criticize the OPI for creating an additional artificial yardstick, the *well-educated* native speaker. They are alarmed by the fact that the performance of the second/foreign learner is judged against an abstract entity that is statistically and normatively derived. In their opinion, the sheer creation of an abstract type of a well-educated native speaker is enough evidence to discredit the OPI as a testing instrument that measures real-life performance.

The opponents of the OPI discussed above recommend that a solid theory of proficiency be developed prior to its implementation in academia and business. They all consider the theory of proficiency that underlies the OPI incomplete, either because of the exclusion of communicative competence as an underlying construct (Savignon 1985; Bachman 1990) or because of its lack of empirical foundation (Lantolf and Frawley 1988). The latter criticize the OPI theory of proficiency as being totally dependent on a proficiency test itself. They point to the circularity in the definition of proficiency: "Proficiency is what proficiency tests measure" (Lantolf and Frawley 1988: 185).

Lantolf and Frawley (1988) insist that a meaningful measurement of oral proficiency should be developed on a solid theory of proficiency that is independent of psychometrics prior to the development of a testing instrument. They write, "Only after such a theory has been developed and is proven to be consistent and exhaustive by empirical research should we reintroduce the psychometric factor into the picture" (Lantolf and Frawley 1988: 185). They assert that the establishment of a theoretical framework of proficiency independent of the test is indispensable for the process of establishing test validity.

Recent critics of the OPI, van Lier (1989), Johnson (1997), Johnson and Tyler (1998), and Johnson (2000), also call for a thorough investigation of the OPI's construct validity. Contrary to Bachman, Savignon, and Lantolf and Frawley, however, they do not insist on developing an external criterion, that is, a theoretical framework, against which the construct of the OPI should be evaluated. They call instead for a thorough examination of the OPI from *within* to determine what it is the OPI measures. They claim that an ethnographic approach to examining the validity of the OPI could yield valuable input for developing a new theoretical framework of speaking ability or modifying the existing models of speaking proficiency.

Van Lier (1989) was the first researcher to challenge the ETS's claim that "a well-structured oral proficiency interview tests speaking ability in a real-life context, a conversation. It is almost by definition a valid measure of speaking ability" (ETS 1982: 13). Van Lier (1989: 494) simply asks, "Is it really a conversation?" Van Lier finds it difficult to accept that the OPI represents an instance of natural conversation, because the ultimate goal of the OPI is not to conduct a conversation but to elicit a ratable sample.

Van Lier (1989) underscores the difference between the discourse of oral interviews and of conversation. Basing his judgment on the Jones and Gerard 1967 model of dyadic interaction, he perceives the discourse structure of the OPI to be more like an interview than a conversation. An interview is characterized by asymmetrical contingency: "The interviewer has a plan and conducts and controls the interview largely according to that plan" (van Lier 1989: 496), whereas a conversation is characterized by terms of mutual contingency dependent on mutual negotiation and equal distribution of rights and duties. Van Lier finds it unclear how the OPI might be able to accommodate both types of contingency within its discourse structure. Although he is more inclined to view the OPI as an interview, he does not exclude the possibility that the OPI discourse structure can represent a different speech event, something else that may fall between two points on the continuum: a conversation and an interview. Van Lier does not name that something else. But the OPI discourse analysis in Ross and Berwick's (1992) study seems to point in the direction of classroom interaction.

Ross and Berwick (1992) initially consider the OPI as conversational exchange between native and nonnative speakers. The types of accommodations employed by interviewers during the OPI, however, suggest to them that the OPI testers' behavior is characteristic of teachers' classroom behavior. In the conclusion of the study they even warn that this type of behavior, teacher's behavior, poses a threat to the validity of the OPI. Although the researchers do not revise their initial assumption about the nature of the OPI discourse, their focus on testers' accommodation behavior introduces a strong possibility that the OPI represents *another* speech event similar to teachers' and students' classroom interaction.

Ross and Berwick's findings are contradicted by Young's (1995a). Young (1995a) modifies the original Jones and Gerard 1967 model of dyadic interaction to analyze the oral data in terms of interactional contingency, goal orientation, and dominance. In his study, he tries to determine whether interviewers' interviewing styles will change when they interact with two groups of learners, advanced and intermediate, who represent disparate levels of speaking proficiency. His findings show that despite variations between the two groups in terms of the amount of talk and the rate of speaking, the behavior of the interviewers, their interviewing style, does not change. The interviewers control the floor, and the learners, whether at the advanced or intermediate level, rarely get the opportunity to initiate a new topic.

The interviewers and interviewees differ as to their goal and dominance. That is, the interviewer's goal does not correspond to the interviewee's goal. Judging by the amount of talking produced by the interviewee, it would seem as if the interviewee dominates the floor. But the interviewee does not have a choice: he/she is required to respond to the interviewer's questions. Thus, dominance in these dyadic interactions is not necessarily a question of speaking more or less or of who initiates more topics; rather, dominance is associated with the goal orientation of the interviewer and the reactiveness of the interviewee.

In an earlier study, Young and Milanovic (1992) also used the Jones and Gerard 1967 model to investigate the discourse of oral proficiency interviews in terms of interactional contingency, dominance, and goal orientation. In addition to these features, Young and Milanovic (1992) investigated the effect of contextual influences, for example, interlocutors, themes, and gender, on the interviewee's performance. They found that tasks, the theme of the interview, and the gender of the participants affected the interviewee's performance. Because these studies are mainly descriptive and exploratory, Young and Milanovic (1992) and Young (1995a) consider their results suggestive rather than conclusive.

Johnson and Tyler (1998) analyzed a representative OPI used widely in official language proficiency tester training workshops to illustrate appropriate techniques and language characteristics of a level 2 speaker. Their analysis reveals that in terms of prototypical aspects of everyday conversation (Sacks, Schegloff, and Jefferson 1974) like turn taking and topic nomination, this particular OPI cannot be considered a valid example of a real-life conversation. Furthermore, their analysis of this particular OPI shows the lack of conversational involvement (Gumperz 1982) on the interviewer's part, which confirms Young and Milanovic's (1992) and Young's (1995) findings pertaining to the interviewer's goal orientation and the interviewee's reactiveness. Like Young and Milanovic (1992) and Young (1995), Johnson and Tyler (1998) caution against generalizing beyond the context of this particular OPI because their findings are based on one OPI.

Johnson and Tyler's (1998) study was originally developed by Johnson (1997) as a pilot study for a larger project aimed at determining whether a model of prototypical features of natural conversation described in the work of Sacks, Schegloff, and Jefferson (1974) could offer some theoretical bases for investigating van Lier's original question: "Is it really a conversation?"

Johnson (1997) recognizes that the question posed by van Lier is critical to the OPI's construct validity. Van Lier rightfully points out that "every manifestation of speaking is speaking in a context, and every contextual manifestation of speaking ability requires, in addition to speaking ability, context-specific skills and experience" (van Lier 1989: 500). If the OPI does not measure speaking ability in the form of conversation, as it claims to do, then the users of the OPI may be misled about candidates' speaking ability.

Furthermore, it may very well be that the OPI has its own unique speech event norms and rules. These norms and rules may not even exist in real life. In that case, the ability to generalize the OPI scores beyond the OPI context could be severely limited. Precisely for these reasons, the investigation of the question, What kind of speech event is the OPI? is of the utmost importance.

Recall that according to Messick (1989), in order to justify a particular inference/interpretation of a test score, we must gather *evidence* for the test's validity and consider the social consequences of such an interpretation. That is, according to Messick's (1989: 13) definition of validity, we need to provide "empirical evidence and theoretical rationales" that "support the adequacy and appropriateness of inferences and actions based on test scores." The next three chapters will be devoted to this process that is, to the process of furnishing theoretical rationales and empirical evidence. In chapter 4, I shall describe *theoretical rationales* for investigating the questions, What kind of speech event is the OPI? and is it really a conversation? In chapters 5 and 6, I shall present *empirical evidence* as to the nature of the OPI communicative speech event.

# Chapter 4

# THEORETICAL BASES FOR INVESTIGATING THE OPI SPEECH EVENT

In this chapter, I shall describe theoretical bases—theoretical rationales, in Messick's term—for investigating the qustion, What kind of speech event is the OPI? Since the key phrase in this question is "speech event," I shall first define that term by referring to the work of Hymes (1972, 1974) and his ethnography of communication. Second, I shall describe various characteristics of the three speech events most frequently associated with the OPI: a conversation, an interview, and a classroom interaction. My description of the selected speech events will be based on recent findings in the field of discourse analysis and on conversation analysis in particular.

By applying discourse analysis methods and techniques to the field of language testing, I wish to advocate the establishment of a closer interdisciplinary connection between language testing and discourse analysis. As the findings of this and the following chapters reveal, such interdisciplinary connection is indispensable for establishing the construct validity of language tests.

## Defining a Speech Event

Hymes (1974) is considered to be the key figure in the development of the ethnography of communication, a field that has strong roots in anthropology and linguistics. Although these disciples have divergent theories and methodologies, they nevertheless have, according to Hymes (1974), one common interest: both linguistics and anthropology are interested in the way people communicate and make sense of the world.

Given that language is the central means by which people communicate, it is important, according to Hymes, to recognize language as a system of rules and behaviors that are an integral part of culture (Hymes 1974; Saville-Troike 1982; Schiffrin 1994). Hymes (1974) elevates language as a system of rules and behaviors to the same cultural status as any other cultural system, political, educational, economic, or whatever.

Hymes presents a functional view of language, which stands in sharp contrast with a structural, or formalistic, view of language like that promoted by Chomsky. Hymes

(1974) lists the main characteristics of these two views of language (table 4.1).

Hymes's (1974) ethnography of communication falls within the functional paradigm, in which language is viewed not as a code but as ways of speaking; in which the structure of language is not grammar but speech act or speech event; and in which linguistic code and language use are seen in dialectical relations. In the functional paradigm, a single homogenous ("idealized") speech community does not exist. Speech community is seen as "organization of diversity," as a gamut of different speech styles.

The goal of the ethnography of communication is to identify and describe communicative patterns and fea-

| *Structural* | *Functional* |
|---|---|
| 1. Structure of language (code), as grammar | Structure of speech (act, event), as ways of speaking |
| 2. Analysis of language structure prior to analysis of use | Analysis of use prior to analysis of language structure |
| 3. Referential function as norm | Variety of social functions |
| 4. Single homogenous speech community | Heterogenous speech community |

Table 4.1   Comparison of a Functional and a Structural View of Language (after Hymes 1974)

tures, which are instrumental for the identification of a variety of types of communicative events. To assist in discovering the properties of communicative events, Hymes developed a classification grid known as the SPEAKING grid, in which the components of the speech situation have been mnemonically arranged to form the acronym SPEAKING (Hymes 1974: 54–66; Schiffrin 1994: 142):

S    *setting:* physical context and circumstances
      *scene:* psychological definition of circumstances
P    *participants:* speaker/hearer
E    *ends:* goals, ends
A    *act sequences:* message form and content
K    *key:* tone, manner
I     *instrumentalities:* choice of medium of transmission of speech (verbal or nonverbal channels)
N    *norms of interaction and interpretation:* specific behavior and properties of speaking and norms of interpretation characteristic for a given cultural system of beliefs
G    *genres:* textual categories, such as poem, myth, lecture etc.

Hymes's SPEAKING grid can be used to discover communicative units that organize the use of language into speech situation, speech event, and speech act. The largest of these communicative units is the *speech situation,* defined as the social circumstances or contexts in which speech occurs. Within the borders of the speech situation the next largest unit is included, namely, the *speech event.*

The speech event is defined as "activities or aspects of activities that are directly governed by rules and norms for the use of speech" (Hymes 1974: 52). The smallest unit of the set is called the *speech act*. Although Hymes does not clearly define what he means by speech acts, Schiffrin (1994: 142) states, "His examples include acts that can be defined through their illocutionary force (e.g., commands, greetings), as well as those that cannot be so defined (e.g., jokes)."

As noted, smaller units are embedded in larger units, and thus within a given speech situation such as a party, *conversation* (speech event) may occur, and within this speech event, a *joke* (speech act) may occur. It is important to point out that all these units are in a reciprocal relationship. That is, each unit helps to define the meaning of another unit while at the same time its meaning is being defined by another unit (Schiffrin 1994). Thus, *questions* (speech acts) in an interview help to define the type of interview (speech event), and the type of *interview* (speech event) sets up expectations as to the type of *questions* (speech act) that are likely to occur (Schiffrin 1994).

The knowledge of the structure and functions of these units—speech situation, speech event, and speech act—constitutes an integral part of native speakers' communicative competence. The notion of communicative competence and several models of communicative competence will be discussed in detail in chapter 8.

To summarize, *speech event* is defined as "activities or aspects of activities that are directly governed by rules and norms for the use of speech" (Hymes 1974: 52). The knowledge of the structure and functions of speech events represents an integral part of native speakers' communicative event. That is, native speakers are able to identify and differentiate among speech events and appropriately adjust their ways of speaking to a given speech event situation.

## Conversation as a Speech Event

In order to investigate the ETS's claim that "the oral proficiency interview tests speaking ability in a real-life context—conversation," the major features of conversation need to be identified and described.

Levinson (1983: 284) defines conversation as "that familiar predominant kind of talk in which two or more participants freely alternate in speaking, which generally occurs outside institutional settings like religious services, law court and the like." Later in the same chapter, while discussing the differences between discourse analysis (DA) and conversation analysis (CA), he states that "conversation is not a structural product in the same way that a sentence is—it is rather the outcome of the interaction of two or more independent, goal-directed individuals, with often divergent interests" (Levinson 1983: 294).

Levinson also distinguishes the unit of conversation from conversational activity. There are many kinds of talk—for example, classroom talk—that exhibit such features of conversational activities as turn taking but that cannot be classified as conversation. A truly spontaneous conversation is "relatively unplannable well in advance. Unlike other forms of discourse, in spontaneous conversation it is difficult to predict the form in which entire sequences will be expressed. The content may be less predictable. Rather, what will be said, the form in which it will be said, and who will say it can be anticipated for limited sequences only (e.g., certain adjacency pairs for certain speaker-hearer relationships)" (Ochs 1979: 57).

Our understanding of the nature and structure of conversational discourse has been advanced by the work of Harvey Sacks, Emanuel Schegloff, and Gail Jefferson, who applied Harold Garfinkel's (1967) approach, known as ethnomethodology, to the analysis of conversation (Schiffrin 1994; Brown and Yule 1983).

Ethnomethodologically based CA is concerned with the problem of social order: how conversation creates its own sense of order and structure and "how language both creates and is created by social context" (Schiffrin 1994: 232). Like ethnography of communication, CA is concerned with speech community members' knowledge; but this knowledge, which pertains to "the way in which participants in talk construct systematic solutions to recurrent organizational problems of conversation" (Schiffrin 1994: 239), is locally shaped and revealed.

CA is reluctant to make premature generalizations or a priori assumptions. The function of such utterances as questions, for example, can only be locally and sequentially determined. The same applies to the CA treatment of the social identity of the participants in conversation and the context in which conversation takes place. Both are text-created and text-revealed (Schiffrin 1994).

The work of Schegloff and Sacks (1973), Sacks, Schegloff, and Jefferson (1974), and Schegloff, Jefferson, and Sacks (1977) has firmly established the highly organized and locally managed system operating within conversation. The local management system, which includes turn-taking, repair, and adjacency pair mechanisms, accounts for patterns of stable and recurrent actions responsible for creating order in conversation.

## The Turn-Taking Mechanism

Sacks et al. (1974) claim that the mechanism that governs the turn-taking system accounts for a small amount of interruption, overlap, and pausing time during conversation. They write, "A basic set of rules governing turn construction, providing for the allocation of a next turn to one party, and coordinating transfer so as to minimize gap and overlap" (Sacks et al. 1974: 704). The turn-taking system provides the answer to how speakers allocate turns and how they know where and when another speaker is about to finish his/her turn.

In Sacks et al. 1974, the turn-taking mechanism is described in terms of two components, the turn construction component and turn allocation component, and a set of rules that apply at the transition-relevance point (TRP). The turn-constructional component is a unit that may include "sentential, clausal, phrasal, and lexical construction" (Sacks et al. 1974: 702). At the end of this unit, called the transition-relevance point (TRP), the transfer of speakers may occur consistent with a set of rules:

1. At the initial transition-relevance place of an initial turn-constructional unit:
   a) If the turn-so-far is so constructed as to involve the use of a "current speaker selects next" technique, then the party so selected has the right and is obliged to take the next turn to speak; no others have such rights or obligations, and transfer occurs at that place.
   b) If the turn-so-far is so constructed as not to involve the use of a "current speaker selects next" technique, then self-selection for next speakership may, but need not be instituted; first starter acquires rights to a turn, and transfer occurs at that place.

  c) If the turn-so-far is so constructed as not to involve the use of a "current speaker selects next" technique, then current speaker may, but need not, continue, unless another self-selects.

2. If at the initial transition-relevance place of an initial turn-constructional unit, neither 1a nor 1b has operated, and, following the provision of 1c, current speaker has continued, then the rule set a–c reapplies at the next transition-relevance place, and recursively at each next transition-relevance place, until transfer is effected. (Sacks et al. 1974: 704)

According to CA, a conversation is locally managed and is produced on a turn-by-turn basis. The turn size, turn order, and turn distribution are not specified in advance; they vary greatly on a case-by-case basis. What participants say is also not specified in advance. The unplanned nature of the event and the unpredictability of outcomes constitute two of the general characteristics of conversation. Moreover, according to Sacks et al. (1974), the turn-taking organization for conversation, in contrast to other speech exchange systems such as interviews, "makes no provision for the content of any turn, nor does it constrain what is (to be) done in any turn" (Sacks et al. 1974: 710).

Sacks et al. (1974: 730) consider conversation as the most natural form of talk and its turn-taking system as the most unconstrained: "It appears likely that conversation should be considered the basic form of speech exchange system, with other systems on the array representing a variety of transformations of conversation's turn-taking system, to achieve other types of turn-taking systems."

## The Repair Mechanism

Closely associated with the operation of the turn-taking mechanism is another central conversational device, the organization of repair. Schegloff, Jefferson, and Sacks (1977) provide a detailed description of the repair mechanism operating in conversation. The authors also make a distinction between correction and repair. Correction constitutes one form of repair and is commonly associated with the replacement of errors or mistakes. Repair, according to Schegloff et al. (1977: 363), is neither "contingent upon error, nor limited to replacement."

The repair mechanism can be divided into two groups, depending on who initiates and who actually performs a repair, and thus can be characterized along the following lines:

1a) Self-initiated repair: repair initiated by the speaker without prompting
1b) Other-initiated repair: repair with prompting
2a) Self-repair: repair done by the speaker of the problem
2b) Other repair: repair done by the other speaker(s).
(Schegloff et al. 1977: 363–65)

Schegloff et al. (1977) also describe a set of ranked preferences for utilization of the repair machinery in conversation. The concept of preference does not refer to a psychological state, but rather to a social organizational notion, and can be related to the linguistic concept of markedness. The preferred organization is unmarked; in contrast, the dispreferred organization is marked (Levinson 1983). The repair system is organized in such a way that the opportunities for self-initiated repair come first, before other-initiated repair opportunities. The set of preferences can be ranked as follows (Schegloff et al. 1977: 363–65):

1. For self-initiated self-repair in the same turn
2. For self-initiated self-repair at transition-relevance point
3. For other-initiated self-repair in the third turn
4. For other-initiated other repair.

## Adjacency Pair

Adjacency pairs represent another local mechanism in conversation. An adjacency pair is a sequence of two utterances produced by different speakers, ordered as a first part and a second part and typed in such a way that a first part requires a particular second part or parts. For instance, greetings require greetings, and offers require acceptance or rejection (Schegloff and Sacks 1973: 296; Levinson 1983:

303; Schiffrin 1994: 236). There is also a basic rule governing the operation of adjacency pair use: "Given the recognizable production of a first part, on its first possible completion its speaker should stop and a next speaker should start and produce a second pair part from the pair type in which the first is recognizably a member" (Schegloff et al. 1973: 296).

Although the adjacency pair represents a fundamental unit of conversational organization, there are also more complex sequential organizations that operate in conversation, for example, insertion sequence, in which questions and answers are embedded within one another (Levinson 1983). The strict criterion of adjacency has been broadened to include the notion of conditional relevance (Levinson 1983): "What the notion of conditional relevance makes clear is that what binds the parts of adjacency pairs together is not a formation of a rule of the sort that would specify that a question must receive an answer if it is to count as a well-formed discourse, but the setting up of specific expectations which have to be attended to" (Levinson 1983: 306).

## Topic in Conversation

Another salient feature of everyday conversation is that topics are spontaneously created and negotiated. Topic is difficult to define because it encompasses different aspects of the communicative process, such as message, code, speaker, or interaction (Schiffrin 1994). Van Lier (1988) also acknowledges the difficulty of arriving at an operational definition of topic. Van Lier points out, however, that this is nothing new in science. In psychology, for instance, there are hypothetical constructs like personality and motivation that "have survived many years of nondefinition" (van Lier 1988: 147). He suggests that the focus in regard to topic should be on *when* is a topic (that is, when a topic begins and ends) rather than *what* is a topic.

The notion of topic in the absence of an operational definition can be regarded as a "pre-theoretical notion of what is being talked about" (Brown and Yule 1983: 71) through some series of turns at talk. In natural conversation, topic is negotiated, and the topical coherence is being "constructed across turns by collaboration of participants" (Levinson 1983: 313). Moreover, in natural conversation there is little focus on topic. Topic emerges spontaneously and, as Ochs (1970: 58) points out, topic is "relatively unplanned and locally managed."

Brown and Yule (1983) agree with Ochs, stating, "It is a feature of a lot of conversation that 'topics' are not being fixed beforehand, but are being negotiated in the process of conversing. Throughout a conversation, the next topic of conversation is developing. Each speaker contributes to the conversation in terms of both the existing topic framework and his personal topic" (Brown and Yule 1983: 89).

Within the existing topic framework that derives from participants' general knowledge, situated context, and the completed part of discourse itself, the researchers distinguish between speaking topically and speaking on a topic (Brown and Yule 1983). Speaking topically refers to the process of making contributions that closely fit the most recent element incorporated in the topic framework. Speaking on a topic occurs when participants concentrate their talk on a particular individual or issue, as during an academic lecture.

One may add that the notion of relevance is closely associated with topical coherence. When talking about relevance, one has to refer to Gricean pragmatics, which is based on the cooperative principle and maxims.

Grice (1975: 45) proposes a general principle, known as the cooperative principle, that participants are expected to observe in the course of their interaction: "Make your contribution such as is required, at the state at which it occurs, by the accepted purpose or direction of the talk exchange in which you are engaged." Grice adds four more specific maxims:

Quantity:
1. Make your contribution as informative as is required (for the current purposes of the exchange).
2. Do not make your contribution more informative than is required.

Quality: Try to make your contribution one that is true.
1. Do not say what you believe to be false.
2. Do not say that for which you lack adequate evidence.

Relation: Be relevant.

Manner: Be perspicuous.
1. Avoid obscurity of expression.
2. Avoid ambiguity.
3. Be brief.
4. Be orderly.

Although these principles are not principles of conversation, but rather of human rational behavior, they provide a basis for inferences about the speaker's intention that may not be code related (that is, that may go beyond the semantic meaning of what has been uttered). The significance of the cooperative principle and maxims is that they assist hearers in making inferences about speakers' communicative intentions.

In summary, the described features of turn taking, repair, adjacency pair, and topic constitute the basic characteristics of everyday conversation. If one accepts the claim of Sacks et al. (1974) that general conversation represents a normal, unmarked system of interaction—a speech-exchange system—and that the turn-taking and repair mechanisms are basic features of conversation, then these features may be used as a framework for investigating how the turn-taking and repair mechanisms in other speech events, such as an interview and a classroom interaction, differ from a conversation, along with other salient features of a conversation such as topic. These prototypical features of everyday conversation (turn taking, repair) along with other salient features of conversation topic thus represent the framework against which other speech events such as an interview and a classroom interaction are compared and contrasted.

## The Interview as a Speech Event

An interview is considered to be a prominent research method in the social and behavioral sciences. It is also a speech event that represents "a powerful force in modern society. Starting almost from birth, we are confronted by questions posed by educators, psychologists, pollsters, medical practitioners, and employers, and we listen to flamboyant interviews on radio and television" (Briggs 1986: 1 cited in Schiffrin 1994: 145).

Van Lier, in questioning the OPI's claim that it measures speaking proficiency in a context of conversation, brings to our attention the notion of asymmetrical distribution of power, a feature typical of an interview. He also identifies five major characteristics of an interview. These characteristics are direct quotations from the work of Silverman (1976) that are, in van Lier's opinion, relevant to the discussion of the OPI as an interview:

1. In a recognizable interview, the scheduled nature of the encounter specifies in advance that what passes will be used to settle future decisions about an issue known prior to the commencement of talk.
2. Interview talk is known to be on the record; that is, the comments of one party will be read as a display of qualities, and this reading will be reported to other persons with a legitimate "right to know" and will eventually produce further decisions.
3. There is some degree of asymmetry in the exchanges between interviewer and interviewee.
4. Questions are provided by one person (or group of persons), and the talk of some other person is to be seen as answers to the questions.
5. One person is solely responsible for beginning and ending the interaction, for ending a topic and introducing a new topic, and for formulating the talk. (Silverman 1976: 142–44, cited in van Lier 1989: 497–98)

Van Lier does not, however, distinguish among different types of interviews, such as survey research interviews, sociolinguistic interviews, and reference interviews (Schiffrin 1994; Mishler 1986). Neither does he mention that interviews differ in terms of Hymes's ends, keys, participants, and their relation to act sequences (Schiffrin 1994).

A *survey research interview* undergoes major scientific scrutiny in Mishler's (1986) *Research Interviewing: Context and Narrative*, which leads to the establishment of several basic characteristics of that type of interviewing. In

Mishler's opinion, a survey research interview is strongly embedded in the behavioristic theory of stimuli and responses in which an interview is viewed as a verbal exchange rather than a form of discourse. This strong behavioristic foundation is connected with a behavioristic definition of an interview: "For our purpose, an interview will be referred to as a face-to-face verbal interchange in which one person, the interviewer, attempts to elicit information or expression of opinion or belief from another person or persons" (Maccoby and Maccoby 1954: 449 cited in Mishler 1986: 9). Kahn and Cannell (1957) also provide a related definition: "We use the term of interview to refer to a specialized pattern of verbal interaction—initiated for a specific purpose, and focused on some specific content area with consequent elimination of extraneous material" (Kahn and Cannell 1957: 16, cited in Mishler 1986: 9).

In a survey research interview, questions and answers are regarded as stimuli and responses. All "extraneous material" is suppressed in order that the findings may be generalized to a larger population. This attempt to emulate positivistic, scientific research leads to interpreting each question and response in isolation, independently of particular features of the context. The context is not viewed as an important factor influencing participants' interaction. The role of the interviewer is to become an expert in stimulus sending, so that the interviewee may become the ideal response emitter.

Moreover, Mishler (1986) points to another typical feature of survey research interviews: the asymmetrical distribution of power. This asymmetry is evident in the interviewer's exclusive control over who will speak, when, and for how long (turn taking), what topics are discussed, and what is relevant and not relevant to the interview. An example of the latter is evident in the frequent suppression of narratives in survey interviews. Narratives, which represent one of the "natural cognitive and linguistic forms through which individuals attempt to order, organize and express meaning" (Mishler 1986: 106), are usually viewed as irrelevant and bearing little contribution to the interview and are therefore suppressed in survey research interviews.

In contrast to survey research interviews, *sociolinguistic interviews* allow for a variety of disparate genres, for example, narrative or description, outside a question-answer format (Schiffrin 1994). Interviewers are trained to avoid the question-answer format and to elicit different types of talk similar to casual conversation. For that reason, sociolinguistic interviews are called "mixed or hybrid speech events" (Schiffrin 1994: 163).

The roles of the interviewer and interviewee in sociolinguistic interviews are also less rigidly defined. Although the asymmetrical distribution of power still exists in sociolinguistic interviews, owing to the fact that the ends (goals) are still hidden from the interviewee, the interviewee is allowed to change roles and ask questions of the interviewers, change and initiate topics, and have greater control over who holds the floor. Different speech events that are allowed to emerge contribute to a better sense of cooperation and solidarity between participants, and thus asymmetry of power is less evident in sociolinguistic interviews.

The distinction among types of interviews is of some importance because it could very well be the case either that the OPI represents one type of interview or that it could accommodate different types of interviews within its internal structure. Thus it could well be that the warm-up and the wind-down phases represent one type of interview and the level check another. Because the type of interaction connected with each described type of interview differs enormously, to claim that the OPI represents an instance of an interview would be too general, too vague, particularly from the testing point of view, in which the generalizability of the scores is the main concern. If the OPI represents a survey research interview, for instance, then the users of the OPI should be informed that the candidate's ability to negotiate topic or to participate in turn distribution is not being assessed. The candidate's score reflects only how well he/she reacts to the interviewers' verbal stimuli.

Despite the differences highlighted above, all interviews share a core feature that allows members of a speech community to interpret them as variants of the same speech event. The core features of all interviews are questions that

are "central to the information-gaining function of all interviews" (Schiffrin 1994: 146).

The central role of questions in interviews does not
mean, however, that questions can be extracted from the
interview itself and analyzed in isolation from the context
in which they occur. As discussed, the communicative
units—speech situations, speech events, and speech acts—
occur within the context of a reciprocal relationship. Their
meaning and interpretation are mutually dependent. That
is, the type and structure of questions are essential for the
understanding of the structure of the speech events in
which they occur, and, in the same way, the structure and
the type of the speech event are essential for the understanding of the type and structure of questions that are
likely to occur in those speech events (Schiffrin 1994).

Schiffrin (1994) used the SPEAKING grid to analyze
two types of interviews (speech events): reference interviews and sociolinguistic interviews. Schiffrin also analyzes
questions (speech acts) which are used in the speech events.
The analysis of these two types of interviews has indicated
that the norms underlying the use of questions are mostly
influenced by the ends and participants in speech events.
The ends and participants have an important effect on the
relationship between questions and act sequences (that is,
message form and content) of the interview. Thus in reference interviews, for instance, questions are primarily
geared to solving a single query or queries (Schiffrin 1994).

Moreover, in the reference interview, the form and function of questions reveal information about the participants' roles and the goals that are associated with their roles: for example, a librarian provides information and the patron seeks information, and both work toward solving a query posed by the patron. The ultimate goal of the reference interview, solving a query, contributes to neutralizing asymmetric distribution of power and knowledge between participants and produces more symmetrical and collaborative efforts on the part of the participants on a turn-by-turn basis (Schiffrin 1994).

In sociolinguistic interviews, Schiffrin (1994) analyzes three types of questions: information-seeking questions, information-checking questions, and clarification questions. The distribution and functions of these questions are also closely tied to the ends and participants in the speech event. For instance, information-seeking questions are used primarily by interviewers. If they are used by the interviewee, they "help to create a change in activity, or genre" (Schiffrin 1994: 169). This change in activity can change the role of the participants and consequently can lead to the emergence of a different type of speech event. What distinguishes the sociolinguistic interview from other types of interviews is precisely its loose internal structure. Sociolinguistic interviews mix the asking and answering of questions with other kinds of talk such as stories, conversation, and so forth.

In sum, questions (speech acts) in an interview provide invaluable information as to the type and structure of the interview (speech event). We can learn more about a speech event on the basis of the questions used in it and vice versa. The mode of questioning allows us not only to distinguish between different types of interviews, but also to influence the way a speech event can be classified or identified, for example, interview or conversation, reference interview or sociolinguistic interview. The relationship between the mode of questioning and speech event constitutes part of native speakers' communicative competence.

This relationship may prove to be useful in providing additional information regarding the OPI speech event.

## Classroom Interaction as a Speech Event

Van Lier (1989) suggests that the OPI may not represent an instance of conversation or even an interview; it may represent something else. This "something else" may be, as indicated previously, connected with the interviewer's behavior. Since most of the OPI testers are teachers of second or foreign languages, it may well be that the OPI represents speech events characteristic of classroom interaction. This requires that the prototypical features of classroom interaction be identified and described so that later on they can be compared and contrasted against the framework of the prototypical features of conversation.

## Overview of L2 Classroom Research

The works of Allwright and Bailey (1991), van Lier (1988), Chaudron (1988), Kasper (1985), and Long and Sato (1983) are of special relevance to our investigation of the nature of the OPI speech event because of their focus on the description and analysis of teachers' and students' interaction in the second language classroom in terms of the Sacks et al. (1974) conversational local management system and in terms of topic (Brown and Yule 1983). The cumulative research of these authors, along with the discourse studies of the Birmingham school (Sinclair and Coulthard 1975), has substantially contributed to identifying the salient features of classroom interaction, which differs from an unmarked system of interaction–conversation, particularly in terms of the previously described framework: the turn-taking mechanism, the repair mechanism, and topic.

## The Turn-Taking Mechanism in L2 Classroom

As with everyday conversation, the sequence of turn taking in the classroom is seldom overtly stated. Rather, it is governed by tacit norms that are followed by the participants in classroom interaction. The existence of those rules becomes obvious when they are violated. It is then typical to hear: "Hold on, it is not your turn," "You will be next," "Raise your hand if you want to talk," and so on (van Lier

1988). Ethnomethodological studies of the turn-taking mechanism in the classroom (McHoul 1978; Kramsch 1985; Chaudron 1988; van Lier 1988; Allwright and Bailey 1991; McCarthy 1991) indicate that turn-taking patterns in the classroom differ from those in general conversation.

Although L2 classroom turn-taking patterns may differ from activity to activity—for instance, pair and group activities will have different patterns—in most class-centered activities self-selection at the transition-relevance point (Sacks et al. 1974) applies only to the teacher. The teacher selects the next speaker and automatically selects himself/herself to follow. There is thus little motivation for students to listen to other students except for fear of being caught off guard without an answer.

The competition as to who holds the floor (which is achieved in conversation by attending to the current speaker's verbal and nonverbal cues and by expressing some personal involvement in the topic) is severely restricted because the teacher has the power to control the turn-taking mechanism. The teacher has the power to assign and terminate the floor, to select the next speaker, and to control the content and thereby the relevance and appropriateness of what is said by the students. In classroom interaction during centralized attention, the speaker's contribution must conform to the pedagogical orientation of the activity.

## The Repair Mechanism in L2 Classroom

The turn-taking mechanism also plays a crucial role in the way the repair mechanism (Schegloff et al. 1977) is observed in the classroom. As noted, in a conversation there is a strong preference for self-initiated self-repair. Even if repair is other-initiated, self-repair is still strongly favored (Schegloff et al. 1977). The strong preference for self-initiated self-repair organization of the repair mechanism in everyday conversation results from other speakers' attempts to avoid the face threats (Brown and Levinson 1987) that might be caused by correction. It may explain why in real-life situations the hearer frequently takes the blame for the speaker's error by pretending that he/she had a hearing problem. It is also important to point out that the propensity for self-initiated self-repair is also observed in native and nonnative conversation outside the classroom setting (Gaskill 1989).

Regardless of the type of classroom, L1 or L2, the classroom repair mechanism differs from the conversational repair mechanism described by Schegloff, Jefferson, and Sacks (1977). As Sinclair and Brazil (1982) indicate, in the L1 classroom interaction there is little chance for students/learners to execute a self-initiated self-repair. When a student makes a mistake, the teacher tends to provide repair before the student gets a chance to initiate his/her self-repair. Sinclair and Brazil's research results are confirmed by Kasper's (1985) findings connected with the investigation of repairs in the L2 teaching classroom. The difference in the repair systems used in the L2 and L1 classroom and in everyday conversation is so drastic that van Lier (1988) proposes a distinction between the conversational repair system and the *didactic repair* system characteristic of the classroom in general.

The description of the L2 classroom repair system may undergo some modification. McHoul (1990) has observed that the teacher withdraws his/her feedback by either creating an opportunity for the student to correct his/her error or by asking another student to provide a correction prior to his/her feedback. This is done by a variety of techniques such as repeating the same question, repeating the student's answer with rising intonation, or other such means. Also, in the classroom the corrected response typically is repeated by the student who made the error. The teacher-initiated repair may occur in the same turn, where it is often perceived as a form of helping the student, or in the next turn, on the completion of a learner turn. In some instances in content-based classroom activity, for example, some students' errors may be left untreated to enable the uninterrupted flow of a particular communicative activity.

Many L2 researchers (van Lier 1988; Allwright and Bailey 1991; McCarthy 1991) have pointed out that the turn-taking and repair mechanisms operating in the classroom deprive students of an opportunity to practice "interactive" behavior typical of a real-life, unmarked form of interaction. Students are simply unexposed to norms of interaction that they will most likely encounter in the environment outside school. In the case of L2 learners, this may lead to miscommunication and social faux pas.

## Topic Negotiation in L2 Classroom

As previously discussed, in natural conversation a topic is negotiated. In contrast, in the classroom topic is rarely negotiated because the focus is not what is talked about, but *how* it is talked about (van Lier 1989). The emergence of a topic that has not been preplanned is usually suppressed by the teacher. In the second language classroom, the teacher elicits information pertaining to a given topic mostly to practice certain linguistic forms, and the teacher holds the sole right to change the topic. Students' involvement in a topic is frequently artificially created by the overall pedagogical goal of the practiced activity (van Lier 1989).

Furthermore, the control of the turn-taking mechanism reinforces the teacher control of the topic, and the feedback move of the basic classroom discourse unit serves as an additional means of controlling the topic. Students' responses are constantly being evaluated and judged not according to what the student says, but according to how he/she says it and how his/her response contributes to the teacher's overall perception of the progress of preplanned topic activity. The feedback to students' answers constitutes probably the major constraint on the occurrence of unplanned and mutually and spontaneously developed topics in classroom interaction (Chaudron 1988; van Lier 1989; Allwright and Bailey 1991).

## Types of Questions in L2 Classroom

L2 classroom research has also led to identification of specific types of questions. It has been observed that the type of questions that most frequently occur in the classroom are *display questions* (Long and Sato 1983; Pica and Long 1986), which request information already known by the teacher, such as, "Are you a student?" This type of question is almost nonexistent in casual conversation. Referential-type questions that are information seeking are typical of casual exchanges (Long and Sato 1983).

Display questions are also called evaluative questions because they set up expectations for evaluative feedback (that is, if the teacher knows the answer, the student expects to get some feedback on whether his/her response was correct or not. In addition, in contrast to casual conversation, in the classroom second language teachers persist in asking questions by repeating or rephrasing them, and they also ask more choice questions (Lightbown 1983).

Long and Sato (1983) distinguish among three types of questions: comprehension check, clarification check, and confirmation check, all of which promote the interaction between native and nonnative speakers. The following examples illustrate each type of question:

Comprehension Check:
He escaped. Do you understand?
Confirmation Check:
NNS: I bought car.
NS: You bought a car?
Clarification Check:
NNS: I bought [bowt] it.
NS: Sorry?

Research (Ellis 1991; Chaudron 1988) indicates that in the L2 classroom the comprehension check is the most frequently employed type of question, to the almost total exclusion of confirmation and clarification checks, which are typical in everyday conversation.

Also, L2 classroom teachers adjust their speech to nonnative speakers in a characteristic way that forms the register known as *teacher talk* (Long, 1983; Long and Sato 1983). The study of teacher talk parallels that of *foreigner talk,* with one exception: in teacher talk, ungrammatical speech modifications and adjustments simply do not occur (Ferguson 1975; Long 1981, 1983).

Formal adjustments occur in both types of speech at all language levels: phonological, morphological, lexical, and syntactic. Such interactional adjustments as comprehension check, confirmation check, and clarification are also typically employed in both types of registers. As noted, however, in the classroom comprehension checks are frequent, and clarification checks and requests for clarification less so. This explains one manner of communication typical of classrooms: the teacher dominates the talk and the students have few opportunities to speak.

In summary, the L2 classroom interaction exhibits some basic characteristics that distinguish this type of speech event from other types of speech events. These characteristics especially apply to the turn-taking mechanism, the repair mechanism, topic negotiation, certain formal language simplifications, and interactional modification.

## Summary of the Prototypical Features of the Three Events: A Conversation, an Interview, and a Classroom Interaction

The following summarizes similarities and differences among the three prototypical speech events: a conversation, an interview, and a classroom interaction:

### The Turn-Taking Mechanism

A conversation is locally managed and is produced on a turn-by-turn basis. The turn size, turn order, and turn distribution are not specified in advance nor is what the participants say. The unplanned nature of conversations and the unpredictability of outcome constitute general characteristics of conversations. In contrast, an interview represents fixed and predictable patterns. The turn size, turn order, and turn distribution are under the interviewer's control. Although the asymmetry of power is less evident in a sociolinguistic interview, in which the interviewee is allowed to change roles—for example, to ask questions)—and to negotiate topic, the interviewer still follows his/her own agenda, a goal that is hidden from the interviewee. In L2 classrooms, the turn order, turn size, and turn distribution are mostly controlled by the teacher. The teacher has the final say as to who will speak, when, and for how long. The teacher has the power to assign and terminate the floor.

## The Repair Mechanism

In conversation, the repair mechanism is organized in such a way that the opportunity for self-initiated self-repair comes before other-initiated self-repair. In sociolinguistic interviews, there is a tendency to use unmarked, conversational-based types of repair mechanisms. In survey research interviews, repairs are more likely to be initiated and provided by the stimuli-sending expert, the interviewer. In the L2 classroom, there is little opportunity for the student to execute self-initiated self-repair. The teacher tends to provide repairs or to ask other students to provide repair. Also, the corrected response is typically repeated by the student who made an error.

## Topic

In conversation, topic is negotiated and unplanned. It emerges spontaneously and is locally managed. In a survey research interview, the interviewer is solely responsible for ending and introducing a new topic. The newly introduced topic may have little connection with what has been previously said. In a sociolinguistic interview, the interviewee has some rights to introduce, or negotiate, a new topic. In the L2 classroom, topic is rarely negotiated because the focus is not what is talked about but how it is said. The teacher holds the sole right to change topic, to suppress the emergence of a topic that has not been preplanned. Also, the teacher's evaluation of the student's remarks hinders the emergence of an unplanned and spontaneously developed topic.

## Question Types

In conversation, one can expect to hear different types of questions intermingled with a variety of different genres such as narrative, anecdotes, jokes, and so on. The core features of all types of interviews are questions, information-seeking questions in particular. In a sociolinguistic interview one may encounter, in addition to questions, different genres similar to conversation. Display questions, typical of the L2 classroom, are almost nonexistent in casual conversation. Also, comprehension check questions are frequently observed in the L2 classroom to the almost total exclusion of confirmation and clarification check questions, which are typical of interviews.

# Chapter 5

# A DISCOURSE ANALYSIS
# STUDY OF THE OPI

In this chapter, I adduce some empirical evidence in the form of quantitative and qualitative OPI data analysis findings. The main purpose of the discourse analysis (DA) study is to answer the questions, What kind of speech event is the OPI? is it most like an everyday conversation, a classroom interaction, or an interview? That is, the ultimate purpose of the DA study is to determine what the most salient features of the OPI speech event are. Once the most salient features of the OPI are identified, we can then match them with the prototypical features of the three speech events described in chapter 4 and thus uncover the prototypical nature of the OPI communicative speech event.

Recall that the proponents of the OPI have argued that it is a valid measure of speaking ability because it represents a real-life context: conversation. But this assertion can be maintained only if careful analyses of OPIs show that they contain the established features of natural conversation. The following study was conducted to test this assertion.

## Data Description

For the purposes of this DA study, thirty-five OPIs, ten each at levels 2, 3, and 4 and five at level 1 were conducted in English by both female and male testers. Originally, forty OPIs were to be selected—ten for each base level; however, because the agency does not keep the records of candidates who do not obtain a level 2 rating, the number of level 1 OPIs was reduced to five. All thirty-five OPIs were audio-taped. Following this federal agency's testing policy, the OPIs were conducted by telephone from the testing head-quarters in Washington D.C. A policy of substituting a tele-phonic OPI for a face-to-face OPI is common in U.S. gov-ernment language institutions. This government agency's official testing policy also requires testers to explain to the candidate the testing procedures, to assure the candidate that his/her opinions regarding different issues will not be held against them, and to explain the reasons for recording the OPI.

All thirty-five OPIs were numbered according to the official rating given to the candidate during the OPI.

The first digit indicates the level of the candidate's proficiency while the last two digits indicate the number of the tape. Thus, 105 indicates that it is a level 1, tape number 5. All thirty-five OPIs, each lasting from thirty-five to fifty minutes, were transcribed according to transcription conventions taken from Schiffrin (1994: 431–32).

## Coding System: A Discourse Analysis Methodology

Because a coding system represents a new methodology for investigating the construct validity of the OPI, I shall describe in detail the steps or stages that have led to its development. The coding system was developed according to the framework described in chapter 4. The ultimate purpose of the coding system was to determine what the salient features of the OPI speech event are.

The development of the coding system proceeded through two major stages. In the first stage, the five major categories of the coding system—turn, repair, topic, question types, and discourse unit—were determined, and their operational definitions were developed. These five major categories were identified to capture the prototypical features of the unmarked form of interaction: conversation against which prototypical features of two other speech events could be compared and contrasted. The subcategories of each of the five major categories were also determined and operationally defined in order to provide answers to the following questions:

> What types of rules apply at the transition-relevance point?
> Who selects the next speaker?
> How is the next turn solicited?
> Who takes the initiative in the distribution of turns?
> Is turn-order fixed or does it vary?
> Is turn-size fixed or does it vary?
> What kinds of "turn construction units" are employed by testers and examinees?
> Who holds the floor most frequently?
> Who controls the floor?

The following represents the operational definitions of a floor turn and its subcategories: turn size and turn allocation followed by examples. The operational definition of a turn in this study was based on Goffman's definition of a turn. Goffman (1981: 23) defines a turn as "an opportunity to hold the floor, not what is said while holding it." The floor turn ends at the *transition-relevance point* (TRP), where the following set of rules applies:

1. Current speaker continues/selects self for the next turn, for example:

> *Cand:* Yes, sir, I learned to speak English in Mexico in school, but at home we spoke Spanish yes I learned to speak English in school . . . *(long pause)* My mother does barely speak English she understand pretty much.

The candidate made a long pause after "yes I learned to speak English in school" that offered an opportunity for the tester to take the floor. Since the tester did not respond, the candidate selected himself for the next turn; he continued to speak.

2. Current speaker selects next speaker for the next turn, for example:

> *Inter: How old is your son?*
> *Cand:* My son is going to turn he's going to be ten in July.

In this example, the current speaker, the interviewer, selects the candidate as the next speaker by posing a question to him.

3. Noncurrent speaker selects self for the next turn, for example:

> *Cand*: I like to go to the movies every week with my friends because I do
> *Inter*: *OK let's change our direction here just a little bit and talk a little bit about current events.*

In this example, the noncurrent speaker selects himself for the next turn by interrupting the candidate and introducing the topic of current events.

In this study, the floor turns were determined and numbered by the author. Basically, change of speakers equals change of floor turn. However, due to the fact that there were many instances of backchannels by the interviewer, in particular, the following two principles were used when determining a floor turn:

1. If during the current speaker's talk, the other participant backchannels without a further attempt to obtain the right to the next turn and the current speaker continues, then such an exchange is assigned to one floor turn. The following example illustrates *one* floor turn assignment:

> *01. Cand:* Well I my my idea what I really wanted to do and that was my original idea ever since I came from Spain was to end up in Washington D.C. but =
> *Inter:* Uh huh
> *Cand:* = I tell you I'm a simultaneous interpreter and that's where the most uh opportunities World Bank and all the big institutions=
> *Inter:* Mm-hm
> *Cand:* = are it's a lot more competitive market but I've I love my profession so I wanted to pursue it.

2. If, however, the current speaker makes a pause at the transition relevance point that allows the other participant(s) to respond and thus self-select himself/herself for the next turn and he/she responds with *Mm-hm,* or *Uh-huh,* then his/her *Uh-huh* is a floor turn in its own right, and not a backchannel, for example:

> *01. Cand:* Yes it's a good idea because it's very important . . . *(long pause)*
> *02. Inter: Uh-huh.*

The candidate's response was assigned to one floor turn and the interviewer's *Uh-huh* was assigned to the second floor turn.

The second major category, *repair,* with its two subcategories, repair type and repair location, was created to provide answers to the following questions:

> What types of repair rules are followed in the OPI?
> Who initiates repairs?
> Who provides a repair?
> Where are initiation and repair located?
> Is the order in which initiation and repair occur fixed or does it vary?

This major category was developed to capture the pattern of repair organization in the OPI. As a reminder, in a casual conversation the preference is for *self-initiated self-repair* in the same turn.

In this study, the category of repair was defined as an attempt by a speaker to alter a trouble source, which was lacking correctness or explicitness. A repair can be self-initiated or other-initiated; it can be self-repaired or other-repaired. Thus, the following types of repair can be observed:

1. Self-initiated self-repaired, for example:

    *Cand:* It was *two o'clock* of your time. No, sorry I meant *three o'clock.*

2. Self-initiated other-repaired, for example:

    *Cand:* And my cousin went to this famous university near San Francisco, Stanford *no no no*

*Inter: Berkeley*

In this example, the candidate realizes that she has provided wrong information. She initiates the need for repair but is unable to provide the repair (that is, give the right name of the university). The repair is provided by the interviewer.

3. Other-initiated self-repaired, for example:

> *Cand:* So my daughter goes to high school. She is *forty* years old.
> *Inter: How old is she?*
> *Cand:* Sorry she is *fourteen* years old.

The candidate mispronounces the word *fourteen*. The interviewer initiates the need for the repair by asking the candidate about her daughter's age. The candidate corrects her previous statement from forty to fourteen.

4. Other-initiated other-repaired, for example:

> *Cand:*.. and you know all those *clutches*
> *Inter*: *What do you mean? I do not understand the last word you just said.*
> *Cand*: Uh: how do you say it? What is this American word for it?
> *Inter: Glitches?*
> *Cand*: Yeah

The candidate mispronounced the word *glitches*. It sounded like *clutches*. Not only did the interviewer initiate the need for repair, but he provided the correct vocabulary as well. Repair may occur within:

1. The same-floor turn, as exemplified in:

   *Cand:* Sorry, I meant *three*

2. At the transition relevance point as exemplified in:

   *Cand:* Stanford . . no no no
   *Inter: Berkeley*

3. In the next floor turn, as exemplified in:

   *Inter:* She is forty?
   *Cand*: No! *Fourteen*

The third major category, *topic,* with its subcategories, was developed to provide answers to the following questions:

> What are the typical features of the OPI topics?
> Are topics spontaneously developed?
> Are topics negotiated?
> Who initiates new topics?
> Who changes topics and how is this change accomplished?

The topic category was thus created to capture the pattern of topic development in the OPI. Recall that in conversation, topics are negotiated, locally managed, and unpredictable. The participants have equal rights to introduce a new topic. No one person is solely responsible for introducing or changing topics.

Three subcategories were created within the topic category: the new topic nomination subcategory was developed to determine whether there is a pattern as to who nominates/introduces a new topic. The topic change natural/

contrived subcategory was developed to determine if a new topic is negotiated or if a new topic is introduced in a similar fashion to a survey research interview. For example, if the previous topic of talk dealt with cooking, a question immediately following regarding the candidate's opinion about his/her stand on abortion would be considered here as contrived. The topic change method subcategory was developed specifically to determine if there is a pattern for how a new topic is introduced. In this study topic change may be introduced by interruption, question, example, and digression.

The *question type* category was developed to obtain additional information regarding types of questions most frequently posed in the OPI. For the purpose of this study a variety of question types were selected. These question types were selected in connection with the three prototypical speech events: a conversation, an interview, and a classroom interaction.

In this study, *information-seeking* questions refer to the question types that seek to obtain information by a participant who lacks the information, for example:

> A: How can I get to your place?
> B: Let me draw you a map.

*Confirmation* questions refer to the question types that seek confirmation from the other interlocutor as to whether his/her utterances were understood correctly, for example:

> A: You said that you want to see me at four, *is this correct?*

*Clarification* questions seek additional information regarding a previous utterance that has not been understood, for example:

> A: I went to cinema?
> B: You went *where?*

*Comprehension check* questions refer to the question types that are used to establish whether nonnative speakers are following what is being said to them:

> A: It was raining cats and dogs. *Do you follow?*

The fifth major category, the *discourse unit,* was developed to provide answers to the following questions:

> What is the OPI basic discourse unit?
> Is the OPI discourse unit similar to a conversation, an interview, or a classroom interaction? or does the OPI have its own unique structure?

The subcategory of *the tester asks question(s), and the candidate answers* was developed to determine if the OPI discourse type unit resembles a prototypical discourse unit of an interview (that is, the interviewer asks questions and the candidate provides answers) as exemplified by turns 19–20 taken from tape 406:

19. *Inter*: What do you remember at that age being the most surprising thing to you [c] perhaps well in a negative or in a positive way. *What was the most difficult thing for you . . the aspect of life in the United States for you to adjust to aside from the language?*

20. *Cand:* Right uh probably the schools because um: I had grown up with a [c] in a Catholic school Catholic German school and the discipline there . . is it's extreme it's it's very strict and I mean you can't even write in notebooks you you get a grade of the grade that you are giving uh reflects on um the discipline that you have with the notebooks and how you deal with your books and when I came here that was the most surprising thing about all the students wrote inside the books and didn't really keep well uh really clean notebooks there. That was the main main thing um and then also racial issues I had never dealt with that in Chile in South America uh um: and just living in a city I guess that was that was very very different from: living in a: very faraway school with the nuns surrounded by nature and then moving to Boston cosmopolitan uh lot of traffic.

In the floor turn 19, the interviewer poses a question, to which the candidate provides a response.

The subcategory of *the tester asks question(s), the candidate answers, and the tester provides feedback* was created to capture a prototypical *classroom* discourse unit. In the prototypical classroom interaction, the teacher asks a question, the student responds, and the teacher provides feedback. This subcategory is exemplified by turns 114–18 in tape 205:

> *114. Inter: Tell me what you've seen what was how would you change a tire, if you had to do it in an emergency.*
>
> *115. Cand:* O.K. if I have to do it?
>
> *116. Inter::* Mm-hm
>
> *117. Cand:* O.K. if I have to do it if I have to do it I think I'll have to get my jack and uh well as far as that goes I I don't have a [c] but probably find a way to do it if I have if it's an emergency then if I had to do it [c] then O.K. put the jack I think there is a little kind of a lever extended somewhere in the jack I put it underneath the [c] and then I pump pump the uh handle hopefully there=
>
> *Inter:* Mm-hm
>
> *Cand:* =is the car is going to go up a little bit and then I will have to get a wrench and uh start removing the screws and uh the screws they=
>
> *Inter:* Mm-hm
>
> *Cand:* =have to [c] all the screws and uh I think basically uh as soon as I get I remove the screws the tire gets loose and then I have I can remove it and if I have a spare tire [c] probably have to check to see if I find a spare tire in my car
>
> *118. Inter:* Okay. Very good.

In floor turn 114, the interviewer poses the question, "How would you change a tire, if you had to do it in an emergency?" to which the candidate responds and after the candidate's response, the tester provides feedback: "Okay. Very good." The subcategory of *the tester and the candidate alternate in asking questions/making comments* was created to capture a prototypical, unfixed, and unpredictable discourse pattern in *conversation*, as turns 31–33 in tape 209 illustrate:

> *31. Inter:* Oh in Virginia, so am I I live in Fairfax County.
> *32. Cand:* Hah, uh. Me too. I live in uh .. west of Springfield.
> *33. Inter:* Oh that is more or less the area I live in. I am in Burke.

## Coding Process

All thirty-five OPIs were coded by the author according to the coding document included in appendix 2. It is important to note that to determine the most salient features of the OPI, an attempt was made to identify three phases in each OPI as well: the warm-up, the level check and probes, and the wind-down phase. The reason for *not* separating the level check and probes was a practical one. Recall that the probes phase is interwoven with the level check, so that the candidate is being alternately stressed and relaxed and not constantly pushed ever higher. That is, from a practical point of view, it would be difficult to separate these two phases; therefore, the decision was made to treat the level check and probes as one phase, and separate it from the warm-up and wind-down phases.

To describe in detail the coding process, one turn (i.e., turn 109 from tape 309) was selected. The following illustrates how turn 109 was coded onto a coding sheet. (For the purpose of this example the coding sheet has been divided into three rows.)

*Tape 309*

109. Inter: Mm-hm all right. And what about health care what would you say about health care if you were a person who wanted more government involvement.

| Floor Turn | Speaker | Turn Unit | Turn Allocation |
|---|---|---|---|
| 109 | 1 | 5 | 2 |

| Repair Type | Repair Location | New Topic Nomination | Topic Natural/ Contrived |
|---|---|---|---|
| — | — | 1 | 1 |

| Topic Change Method | Question Type | Discourse Unit |
|---|---|---|
| 2 | 1 | 1 |

Figure 5.1    An Example of the Coding Process

Turn 109 belongs to the tester. This is indicated by the number 1 under the Speaker category. The number 5 under the category of Turn Unit indicates that the tester asked a question. By virtue of asking a question, the tester selected the candidate as the next speaker, which is indicated by the number 2 under the Turn Allocation category. There is no repair in this turn, so the category Repair Type and Repair Location do not show any number. The tester initiates a new topic of health care, which is indicated by the number 1 under the Topic Nomination category. The topic of health care is connected with the topic discussed previously in turns 107 and 108, and therefore the new topic introduced by the tester was coded as 1 (i.e., Natural). The method of introducing a new topic was in the form of a question, which is reflected by the number 2 under the category of Topic Change Method. The number 1 under the category of Discourse Unit indicates that the tester asked a question which was followed by the candidate's response in turn 110.

Frequency counts of the coded OPIs and chi-square statistics were performed to provide answers to the following questions:

> When the tester holds the floor, what is the most frequent/typical floor turn size?
> What is the tester's most typical method of obtaining the floor?

What is the tester's and the candidate's most typical
way/method of obtaining the floor?
What is the most typical repair method?
What is the most typical repair location?
Who most frequently nominates a new topic—the
tester or the candidate?
When a new topic is nominated, is it Natural or Con-
trived?
What is the most typical method/way of introducing a
new topic by the tester and by the candidate?
What is the most typical question type posed by the
candidate and by the tester?
What is the most typical discourse unit of the OPI?

Readers are encouraged to refer to Johnson (1997) for the
results of chi-square statistical analyses. In the following
section, I shall summarize the findings of the DA study for
each of the major categories.

## Summary of the Findings of the DA Study for Each of the Major Categories

### Distribution of Turn

When the tester holds the floor, a straightforward *question*
is the most typical turn unit. In contrast, the candidate's
most frequently used turn unit is an *utterance*. Questions
are relatively infrequently used by the candidate. There is a
predictable pattern as to the tester's and the candidate's behavior in terms of turn unit. Whenever a question is posed,

one may predict that the tester poses it, and whenever a response in terms of utterance(s) is given, it will be uttered by the candidate. This pattern does not change with the candidate's level of proficiency. Regardless of proficiency level, the tester is most likely to ask questions and the candidate is most likely to provide responses. This pattern contradicts one major prototypical characteristic of conversation that the OPI claims to represent. Recall that in conversation, turn unit type (along with turn location and turn distribution) is unpredictable; it is not fixed.

## Turn Allocation

The most typical way for the candidate to obtain the floor is to be directly nominated by the tester. When the candidate finishes the response, the turn goes back to the tester, who has the right either to accept it or give it back to the candidate to continue. The latter is signaled by frequently used backchanneling. Thus, when the candidate returns the turn to the tester he/she does so indirectly, simply by completing his/her response. This pattern of turn allocation can be illustrated as follows:

> Tester selects the candidate as the next speaker directly by posing questions/tasks/role-plays;

> Candidate selects the tester as the next speaker indirectly. That is, after his/her response is completed, the turn goes back to the tester.

This pattern of turn allocation is observed at all levels of proficiency and is illustrated by the following excerpt from tape 201:

> 15. *Inter: How long does it take exactly to to get from Salt Lake to Provo?*
> 16. *Cand:* I took a bus this morning so it took me about an hour and twenty minutes to get here.
> 17. *Inter: Oh you rode the bus?*
> 18. *Cand:* Yeah I did.
> 19. *Inter: Did they have a good bus service from between the two cities?*
> 20. *Cand:* Yeah they have UTA Utah Transit Service and it's real good.
> 21. *Inter: (clears throat) What kind of buses are they uh do they have? Are they big ones?*
> 22. *Cand:* It's really big one.
> 23. *Inter: Oh I see I see. Interesting! Now, is there any kind of train connection between the two cities?*
> 24. *Cand:* Uh [c] usually I I think they do but I never take a train. They have Amtrak from Provo to Salt Lake and: I don't know how much it costs but they have it have a Amtrak [c] from Provo to Salt Lake.
> 25. *Inter: Now, (clears throat) you say that you have lived in Provo for four years now?*
> 26. *Cand:* Yeah
> 27. *Inter: Is that the only place in Utah that you've lived?*
> 28. *Cand:* Yeah, I came I came here in nineteen .. ninety.
> 29. *Inter: Oh nineteen ninety. And from where did you come?*

In this excerpt, the tester selects the next speaker (the candidate) directly by asking questions:

> Turn 15: How long does it take exactly to to get from Salt Lake to Provo?
> Turn 17: Oh you rode the bus?
> Turn 19: Did they have a good bus service from between the two cities?
> Turn 21: What kind of buses are they uh do they have? Are they big ones?
> Turn 23: Now, is there any kind of train connection between the two cities?
> Turn 25: Now, (clears throat) you say that you have lived in Provo for four years now?
> Turn 27: Is that the only place in Utah that you've lived?
> Turn 29: Oh nineteen ninety. And from where did you come?

The candidate selects the tester indirectly. That is, after his/her response is completed, the turn goes back to the tester. This predictable pattern stands in sharp contrast to what one may expect to observe in a real-life conversation. This predictable pattern of turn allocation points in the direction of an interview in which the interviewer is expected to be in total control over the turn distribution.

## Repair

Although the chi-square results for this major category are not significant based on the raw numbers alone, it seems that the most preferred method of repair in the OPI both for the tester and the candidate is *self-initiated self-repair,* which is performed within the same turn. The following illustrates this preference:

> *Cand:* But I know that during the summer it's very hot *at* sorry *in* Washington also.

It seems that the pattern of repair in the OPI is similar to that in conversation, in which there is a preference for self-initiated self-repair in the same turn. Interestingly, based on the raw numbers, there seems to be a rather low frequency number of repair in the OPIs. This is rather striking considering the fact that the interaction is between native and nonnative speakers. This may be explained by the OPI testing procedure, according to which testers are discouraged from providing the candidate with corrective feedback. Testers are trained to ignore the candidate's request for assistance with vocabulary or grammatical structure. Within the OPI context, the candidate's linguistic shortcomings represent an important clue as to the candidate's level of proficiency. Also, specific types of error are identified for each level to assist the tester with proper and efficient assessment of the candidate's level of proficiency. This explanation, however, should be treated as a conjecture. Further research is needed to determine its validity.

## Topic Nomination

If a new topic is introduced, the person most likely to introduce it is the tester. In the OPI, the tester is in control of changing topic and thus of determining what will be and what will not be talked about. The topic change introduced by the tester is most typically *contrived,* as opposed to the candidate's topic change. The tester tends to follow his/her own *agenda.* The change of topic on the tester's part has little to do with what has been discussed previously. This pattern is observed across the OPI levels. The following excerpts taken from level 2 and level 3 OPIs illustrate the claim mentioned earlier, namely, that the tester follows his/her own agenda:

*Tape 202*

*149. Inter: Do you um the room that you're in what do you see when you look around that room? Describe that for me please.*

150. *Cand:* Okay in front of me the telephone with also lot number on it and they have like menu data [c] and all of those and have also have phone number for this phone on the phone. Uh Okay beyond that they have a black tape recorder and they no there is no tape in it uh on the left side there is a typewriter . . Okay over the desk and that have three drawers . . Okay on the left side far the corner of my room where I am sitting uh there's a a shelf that's a lot of papers on them . . Okay for example

> all the applications and [c] that and uh on the back
> where I sit there's uh some hangers I hang we will
> hang coats and on it and my back the right the cor-
> ner back there is a TV and a VCR. Uh that's all.
> *151. Inter: Okay okay I'd like for us if we can to talk
> just a little about Southeast Asia.*

In this excerpt taken from tape 202, the tester poses
questions that are aimed at eliciting level-specific tasks. In
turn 149, the tester's question, "Do you um the room that
you're in what do you see when you look around that
room" is aimed at eliciting a task of description, which is a
required task for level 2. The tester's next question, "I'd like
for us if we can to talk just a little about Southeast Asia" introduces another level 2 task (a current event task), which
has little to do with what has been discussed previously.

A similar pattern can be observed in the next excerpt taken from tape 308:

> *107. Inter:* Okay. Uh in the newspaper today it said
> something about uh it's not easy to be an immigrant
> in the United States. *Immigrants were victims in
> their country and now they're victims here. Tell me
> uh why immigrants are victims*
> *108. Cand:* Well uh I believe there is some uh some de-
> gree of prejudice towards foreigners specially people
> right away uh notice for example even if you speak
> the language if you have any kind of accent they
> kind of uh not [c] I feel that that they may treat you
> different also I I've noticed that here appearances
> count very much so they're they see you for ex-

ample if they see you are dark complexioned they assume immediately or most of the time that you're an immigrant and you may not [c] for example. You may be a second- or third-generation American still you you face that that burden prejudice.

*109. Inter:* Mm-hm and uh do you think that uh people are really victims?

*110. Cand:* Well no I think that although you're if you really want to assimilate you have a very good opportunity to uh improve yourself and to achieve a good lifestyle. I think there's more opportunity here.

*111. Inter:* Mm-hm

*112. Cand:* For people that really cares for for being educated and for working than in other countries.

*113. Inter:* Mm-hm. Okay I'll give you another question now. Okay?

*114. Cand:* Mm-hm

*115. Inter:* Uh *if you could buy a car any car in the world uh which one would you get would you get an expensive uh or a beautiful one uh would you like something like a Volvo or what kind of car would you buy?*

In this excerpt, after the topic of immigration (turn 107) the tester introduces the topic of buying a car (turn 115), which has little to do with what has been discussed previously.

These excerpts seem to indicate that a new topic is not negotiated, but controlled by the tester. The tester, *not* the candidate, has a right to say, "Okay I'd like for us to talk about Southeast Asia," "Okay I will give you another question," or "Okay very good, next question." The tester, not the candidate, has a right to introduce a topic that has little relevance to what has been discussed previously. This treatment of topic contradicts the ETS's claim that the OPI is conversational in nature.

## Question Types

The most typical question type posed by the tester is information seeking, followed by information checking. The most frequently posed question by the candidate is clarification. This pattern is consistent for all levels of proficiency. That is, when a clarification question is posed, one may safely predict that this type of question was most likely posed by the candidate rather than the tester.

## Discourse Unit Type

The OPI's most typical discourse unit is: *the tester asks a question and the candidate answers* (and its variation: the tester presents a task/role-play, which substitutes a question, and the candidate answers) that, as you recall, was originally developed to capture a prototypical discourse unit of an interview that the OPI may represent. This discourse unit is primarily associated with the level check and probes phases.

The second most typical discourse unit is: *the tester and the candidate alternate in asking questions/making comments,* which was originally developed to capture a prototypical discourse unit of a conversation that the OPI may represent. This discourse unit is typically associated with the warm-up and the wind-down phases. The findings of the DA study point in the direction of the OPI speech event as an interview. Schiffrin (1994: 146) writes that the core feature of all types of interview are questions that "are central to the information gaining functions of all interviews." And, indeed, the most typical discourse unit originally designed to capture the interview-like nature of the OPI is: the tester asks question(s), the candidate answers. However, the existence of another discourse unit, which is closely associated with the warm-up and the wind-down phase, indicates that the OPI represents two types of interviews: a sociolinguistic interview, in which some instances of conversation-like interaction can be observed, and a survey research interview, which represents a verbal exchange based on a behaviorist foundation of stimuli and responses.

## The Level Check and Probes as a Survey Research Interview

The picture that emerges from the discourse analysis is that the level check and probes represent a very formal type of interview. These phases of the OPI seem to represent a formal verbal exchange, not a discourse form (Mishler 1986).

In this formal verbal exchange, not only does the tester control when and for how long the candidate will hold the floor, but also the topic the candidate will talk about. The role of the tester/interviewer is to provide a stimulus (a question or a task), and the role of the candidate/interviewee is to respond. There is little negotiation allowed on the part of the candidate. The following examples taken from various OPIs illustrate the view of the level check and probes as a verbal exchange. The first example is taken from tape 403:

*Tape 403*

244. *Inter:* Okay let's imagine this say he asks you you talked you tell me you talked about immigration I don't understand that word. Explain that to me daddy.

245. *Cand: Well I don't think my son is uh at the stage where he knows about immigration yet.*

246. *Inter:* Is there any way you can think of for me that that you might try to tell him what immigration is?

247. *Cand: At three years* ⌈old⌉

248. *Inter:*                    ⌊If  ⌋ he hears you say that word how would you tell him or you could say
                                    ⌈you could exp⌉

249. *Cand:*                        ⌊Yeah I know what you⌋ mean like if he keeps uttering that word all the time=

250. *Inter:*                              Yeah⌋

251. *Cand:*                                      = and he wants to know the meaning of [c] immigration?

252. *Inter:* Yeah!

253. *Cand: Although I'm not assuming that he will utter that word all the time because it well let's assume that he is uttering* so I would always explain to him immigration as as his father his father immigrated to this country. I came from a different country to uh this country or immigration is like to come from another country into another country.

This excerpt illustrates the candidate's limited power of negotiation of a new topic/task. Despite his objection as to the "validity" of the task presented to him (the candidate clearly finds its improbable that his three-year-old son will ask for an explanation of the word *immigration*), the candidate is forced to respond. His comments regarding the credibility of the task are totally ignored by the tester, who acts as if he has a right to "do" whatever he finds important to his own agenda. He will not change the task even though the candidate's objections make sense because it would mean giving up his power.

Some questions posed by testers in the level check and probes phases are so formal and so unrelated that they sound as if they had been prepared ahead of time, as if they were being read by the tester. As an illustration, consider tape 402: after the discussion of the topic of buying a new car (turn 117), the interviewer introduces the topic of immigration (turn 137) followed by the topic of militant groups (turn 139) followed by the topic of education (turn 145):

*Tape 402*

*117. Inter:* Uh-huh. Okay! Good. Uh if you: *were to buy a car uh what kind of a car would you get?* Would you buy an expensive one a beautiful one or a well-made one?

*137. Inter: Uh-huh. Good. Okay. Very good. Uh next question.* Uh we hear a lot about immigration these days in the news uh many problems many uh uh comments by different people. Uh immigrants themselves feel that in this country they're not treated well. And they feel like they are victims. Uh could *you tell me why you think uh uh immigrants feel like they are victims in this country?* They were victims where they came from and [c] now when they come here they feel like victims. *Could you tell me why you think they feel that way?*

*139. Inter:* Uh-huh. Okay. Uh did you read this uh weekend about that those *militant groups uh in our country* who uh claim to dislike uh: our government and they feel that uh uh: they uh now these are not immigrants but they're unhappy with the situation [c] with the government here. Uh I I was thinking uh do you think that people should stay in this country if they're unhappy with the government? *I'm talking about these militant people [Laughs]. Do you think they should stay if they stay?*

*145. Inter:* It's interesting to hear their comments. Uh Okay: uh uh twenty-five years ago there was a court case called Brown versus the Board of Education and the phrase that they used a lot was *"separate but equal" Uh do you know what that means?*

In many instances, the tester's topic selection sounds rather challenging and insensitive. The candidate frequently expresses his/her discomfort (detected in her/his voice, longer pauses, and so on) while providing the answer to the tester's stimuli—questions. This is illustrated in turn 177 tape 205 and turn 137 tape 402:

*Tape 205*
*177. Cand:* Okay all right *uh uh uh:* I think that uh my the first thing that *uh: uh* really comes to my mind when *uh uh* I I am I'm *uh uh* I agree on abortion in case of the following, uh case of rape *uh:* in case of a very after a thorough examination by several specialists that the the fetus *uh uh:* the young fetus that I had or somebody had *uh uh* is very deformed and the likelihood that he is the baby will live for y'know a short period of time is very unlikely then I would consider an abortion for that *uh uh:* and the other case is when the mother's *uh uh uh* the mother's *uh uh: uh* life is in danger and Okay I think *uh*

In this excerpt, the candidate is asked to express her opinion about abortion. From her tone of voice, it is evident that the candidate does not feel comfortable taking about this topic. In addition, her arguments are challenged by the tester, who in turn 178 expresses her dissatisfaction with the candidate's stand on abortion: "Just *those* two circumstances?"

*Tape 402*
*137. Inter: Uh-huh. Good. Okay. Very good. Uh next
question.* Uh we hear a lot about immigration these
days in the news uh many problems many uh uh
comments by different people. Uh immigrants themselves feel that in this country they're not treated
well. And they feel like they are victims. Uh could
*you tell me why you think uh uh immigrants feel
like they are victims in this country?* They were victims where they came from and [c] now when they
come here they feel like victims. *Could you tell me
why you think they feel that way?*

Considering the fact that the candidate is an immigrant
himself, this question puts the candidate in an awkward,
somewhat defensive position. The question seems to imply
that all immigrants feel like victims and he, being an immigrant, has "inside" information why "they feel that way."

Some testers often explicitly tell the candidate that
they do not have to "tell the truth" while expressing their
opinions about a given topic, as illustrated in turn 170 tape
205: "You don't have to tell me your real views on this
okay, just make them up," and in turn 61 tape 207: "so
you may say to me exactly what your opinion is. You
make something up that's contrary to what you actually
feel." This stands in sharp contrast to what participants in
a real conversation are expected to do:

*Tape 205*
*170. Inter:* Okay. Good. Okay uh let's go on to another question. Okay uh this is on abortion, okay,

*you don't have to tell me your real views on this okay just make them up.* In your opinion what circumstances should exist before a physician or a doctor suggests to his patient that she should consider an abortion

*Tape 207*

61. *Inter:* A little bit later on but the thing I want to stress to you about all this is that I'm not going to be judging you on your opinions my only purpose in asking you all these things is to get you to use spoken English *so you may say to me exactly what your opinion is. You make something up that's contrary to what you actually feel that is not important to me at all.*

The disconnected nature of the tester's questions within the level check and probes phases, combined with the type of questions that focus on grammar, give an impression that this phase of the OPI represents a language test in which the candidate's grammar and vocabulary are being tested. The following excerpt from tape 301 illustrates this point:

93. *Inter:* But I'd like for you to imagine that I have never been to a soccer game before and *I want you to give me a brief idea of what the game consists of and what the rules are how one plays soccer.*
94. *Cand:* Well it's basically I mean you're going to use your your your foot in all uh parts of the game your foot and head you can't touch it with your hands and uh it's it's each team consists of eleven

players one goalie and eleven outside player [c]. Uh there's defense and mid-field and offense and and the goal is to try to score as many goals in the opponents' goal as possible it's not a fast going game and uh there's a lot of [c] involved if uh if you had a chance to look at any soccer games before. Uh: uh what else hm that's I'm sure there's a lot of technical

95. *Inter:* Do you think that soccer as a sport requires more finesse and maybe intelligence than American football?

96. *Cand:* They both require intelligence it doesn't require more finesse no not really there is a lot of y'know interaction between players too of course not like football you're not trying to bring somebody down on the floor but (laughs) but uh: there is more maybe tactics in soccer yeah than football. But each one has its beauty in its own different way.

97. *Inter:* I want you to imagine that I'm a friend of yours who has just come from Egypt and I've been reading a newspaper article and: in the article it's about a criminal case they talk about *plea bargaining.* How would you explain this term to me? Does it mean that I I even though I speak English I'm just not familiar with this term.

98. *Cand:* Plea bargaining?

99. *Inter:* Right

100. *Cand:* Uh-huh.

101. *Inter: How would you explain a plea bargain to me?* Is [c]

102. *Cand:* I'm not really familiar with it that much too I mean. Plea bargain uh um the term itself you talking about some bargaining his uh I mean uh

*103. Inter: Or let's suppose I've been reading an article about counterfeiting. What how would you explain that to me what counterfeiting is? If something is a counterfeit what does that mean?*
*104. Cand: I mean it's it's not legit it's like counterfeiting money for example? Or it's it's*
*105. Inter: But what does one do if one is a counterfeiter. What what is the process? What happens?*
*106. Cand: (laughs) Well you're trying to produce uh money that's not really y'know uh uh that's fake and it's illegal. Uh: that's basically what it is I the process itself I mean you just what is it called you're publishing money or whatever to do things that are not legal.*

Here, typically for the level check and probes, the tester switches abruptly from the topic of sports (playing soccer) to questions that clearly test the candidate's knowledge of vocabulary. Considering the fact the tester is a native speaker of English, the question ("Or let's suppose I've been reading an article about counterfeiting. How would you explain to me what counterfeiting is?") sounds artificial. Had the tester changed the agent of reading from herself to the candidate's Arabic friend who does not understand this English word, for instance, the task might have sounded more realistic.

In the level check and probes phases, the tester frequently makes evaluative remarks prior to introducing a new topic/task/role-play situation. These explicit remarks serve as a reminder to the candidate that this is not a conversation. The following excerpt from tape 303 illustrates these points:

> 69. *Inter: Let me ask you this question* also if I may and I want to emphasize for you before you even answer that it is asking going a little bit into your personal life but I am not prying into that. I have a *linguistic reason* why I want to ask you this question and here it is. We are of course at the beginning of the week now this is Monday and we've just come off the weekend. Could you briefly tell me how you spent the weekend starting from Friday night or Saturday morning until last night.

The phrase "Let me ask you this question," combined with "I have a linguistic reason," sends a signal to the candidate that he is not being engaged in a casual conversation, but that his language skills are being assessed. Also, the tester's explanation as to his expectation:

> *The test* doesn't have anything to do with your opinions. All right. What would you say how what your views you hold have no effect on *the grade*. It's it's how you express yourself exactly. You can feel free to say anything you want in any way you want to say as long as as long as *the language is correct*

contradicts the notion that the OPI is a conversation. The following excerpt from tape 208 illustrates the same point: the OPI is a language exam, not a conversation:

*156. Inter:* I should have mentioned it in the beginning
of *the exam* we got =
*Cand:* Uh-huh
*Inter:* = we got into things so quickly that I didn't
mention it uh-huh that *the test* doesn't have anything to do with your opinions. All right. What you
say how what your views you hold have no effect
on the *grade.* It's it's how you express yourself exactly. You can feel free to say anything you want in
any way you want say as long as as long as *the language is correct.* So you know it I whether you are
for this or against that or you do this or don't do
that that's not that's not an issue in this uh Okay

The level check phase is the most important for the
process of the OPI rating. Some testers even make very explicit remarks that separate this phase from the warm-up
phase, which has little impact on the outcome of the OPI
rating. The following portion of the OPI, tape 303 illustrates this point. After a rather lengthy discussion of the
weather, which seems to be the most popular topic of the
warm-up and the wind-down, the tester gives an explanation of the agency's testing procedures. The first sentence
of the tester's explanation of the testing procedures is very
revealing. It explicitly states that what has been discussed
up to this point is apparently irrelevant:

*Tape 303*
*52. Cand:* Yes, I was born and raised most of my life
right here on the border.

53. *Inter:* On the border, huh?

54. *Cand:* It's a small town close to McAllen which name is Reynosa.

55. *Inter:* Reynosa. Okay

56. *Cand:* Yes.

57. *Inter:* I've never been to that part of well I've never even been to Texas at all unfortunately . . I hear it's a a very interesting state with lots of things to do lots of things to do and see and I would really like to visit one of these days.

58. *Cand:* Okay Uh: well I never returned to my original place where I live which is the capital, Mexico City. I never return and (laughs) but I would like to return and visit especially those historical places and remember my culture it's a beautiful culture there are very beautiful architecture old historical places like the Parliament and all uh those uh places. It's nice to be there and make a trip.

59. *Inter: You and I sir are going to be talking in English for just a while a little while this afternoon* and after we finish I'll turn you over to uh what we'll do is we'll hang up and then then you'll be speaking in your foreign language conversation for a while. But concerning both tests let me give you a little bit of information a little bit of information if I may.

After a lengthy warm-up phase, the tester's remark: "You and I sir are going to be talking in English for just a while a little while this afternoon" sounds out of place. It contradicts what they have been doing so far. They have been talking in English for some time now, but apparently it does not have any effect on the process of rating. The real talk in English will begin as of the next phase—the level check. The tester's remarks seem to serve as a signal to the candidate. As of now, the candidate needs to be careful how he speaks in English.

To summarize, the findings of the discourse analysis for the level check and probes point toward a very formal type of interview, a type of interview that falls under Mishler's category of a survey research interview. The definition of a survey research interview seems to capture the essence of the interaction in the level check and probes phases: "An interview will be referred to as a face-to-face verbal interchange in which one person, the interviewer, attempts to elicit information or expression of opinion or belief from another person or persons" (Maccoby and Maccoby 1954: 449, cited in Mishler 1986: 9). "We use the term *an interview* to refer to a specialized pattern of verbal interaction—initiated for a specific purpose, and focused on some specific content with the consequent elimination of extraneous material" (Kahn and Cannell 1957: 16 cited in Mishler 1986: 9). All "extraneous" material is suppressed in order that the findings may be generalized to a larger population, so that the OPI results can be, in the words of one of the testers, "standardized throughout the federal government." This attempt to emulate scientific research leads to interpreting each question and response in isolation, independently of particular features of context. The lack of context may explain why the tester's questions sound so disconnected. This may also explain why the tester feels justified in asking a question about the candidate's favorite dish immediately followed by a question about abortion. The role of the tester is to be an expert in sending stimuli so that the candidate may become the ideal response-emitter. The tester's role is to elicit "a fair sample" of spoken language, not to conduct a conversation. The level check and probes also exhibit another typical feature of a survey research interview (that is, a verbal exchange based on a behaviorist foundation of stimuli and responses): the asymmetrical distribution of power. This asymmetry is evident in the tester's exclusive control over when and for how long a speaker holds the floor, what topics are to be discussed, and what is or is not relevant to the interview. The following examples from the transcribed OPI data illustrate this asymmetry of power within the level check and probes phases. The tester has the power to interrupt the candidate in any place he/she considers relevant, as turn 136 in tape 409 illustrates:

> 135. *Cand:* Second I would immediately implement as part of the school uh: schedule one course uh uh maybe daily half an hour a day or one hour a day or or whatever to the school's schedule uh: on educating children about weapons and about violence and giving them statistics and showing them uh movies and the same way that these children are being taught to be violent how carrying weapons to school how gangs are cool well we should show them also

the other side of the coin I believe this should be also part of the school's program. I think it should be part of the education and I think the only way children are going to: stop imitating is if they understand we can't force anything into anyone and nobody learns with somebody else's

*136. Inter: Okay let's just shorten it right here and switch gears just a little bit same subject only now you're talking to your son.*

The candidate in turn 135 responds to the task presented to her by the tester in the preceding turn, in which she was asked to address the school board regarding the subject of safety in schools. Her argument for the ban of guns or weapons in schools is interrupted by the tester in turn 136: "Okay lets just shorten it right here and switch gears just a little bit," and she is given another task.

## The Warm-up Phase and the Wind-down Phase as a Sociolinguistic Interview

According to Sacks et al. (1974), the turn size, turn order, and turn distribution are not specified in advance in conversation. Moreover, according to Sacks et al. (1974: 740), the turn-taking organization in conversation, in contrast to other speech exchange systems such as an interview, "makes no provision of the content of any turn, nor does it constrain what is (to be done) in any turn." Topic in conversation emerges spontaneously and, as Ochs (1970: 58) points out, topic is "relatively unplanned and locally managed." The discourse analysis indicates that the warm-up and the wind-down phases have a typical discourse unit in common, which distinguishes them from the level check and probes. Although they contain more conversation-like features, the controlled nature of turn taking and lack of topic negotiation prevent these two phases from being viewed as everyday conversation. The combination of conversation-like features and interview-like features exhibited in the warm-up and wind-down points in the direction of a more conversation-like type of an interview, a type similar in nature to the interaction in a sociolinguistic interview.

Recall that a sociolinguistic interview allows for a variety of different genres, such as narrative and description, outside a question-answer format (Schiffrin 1994). To conduct an appropriate sociolinguistic interview, interviewers are trained to avoid the question-answer format and to elicit different types of talk similar to casual conversation. For that reason, sociolinguistic interviews are called "hybrid speech events" (Schiffrin 1994: 163). The roles of the interviewer and interviewee in sociolinguistic interviews are expected to be less rigidly defined than in survey research interviews.

Although the asymmetrical distribution of power still exists in sociolinguistic interviews, the interviewee has greater control over who holds the floor. The interviewee is allowed to ask questions and negotiate a new topic. This contributes to a better sense of cooperation and solidarity between the interviewer and the interviewee and thus makes the asymmetry of power less evident. Overall, in sociolinguistic interviews, the interaction is more locally managed. That is, it is managed on a turn-by-turn basis with the interviewer more closely adhering to what has been said previously. The following examples of the warm-up and wind-down phases illustrate these points in support of the claim that the warm-up and wind-down phases represent a sociolinguistic interview:

*Tape 209*

25. *Inter*: Oh I see, I see, so that's your native language?
26. *Cand:* Yes.
27. *Inter:* Oh uh how long have you been in the United States?
28. *Cand:* Since 1981.
29. *Inter:* Are you in the Virginia suburbs or the Maryland suburbs?
30. *Cand:* I'm in Virginia.
31. *Inter: Oh in Virginia, so am I I live in Fairfax County.*
32. *Cand:* Me too. I live in uh west of Springfield.
33. *Inter: Oh that is more or less the area I live in. I'm in Burke.*
34. *Cand:* We are right close to Burke, anyway.

In this excerpt taken from tape 209, the tester offers some personal revelation. Both the tester and the candidate contribute to the topic, which is locally managed. The pattern of question/response is not so prevalent as in the level check and probes phase. Also, the candidate is allowed to change role (to ask questions of the tester) as the following example from tape 308 illustrates:

*Tape 308*
27. *Inter:* I like it very much. You know you know what I didn't know about that hotel that they gave you free breakfast.
28. *Cand:* Yes
29. *Inter:* And I paid for it for a month.
30. *Cand:* Oh really?
31. *Inter:* (laughs) And nobody told me it was for free. And then one day someone told me and I told them I wanted my money back and they said I couldn't have it back.
32. *Cand:* Wow.
33. *Inter:* So I wrote to the owner of uh of the Hilton chain and I said I wanted to be reimbursed for that money was about a hundred dollars you know (laughs)
34. *Cand:* Well were you?
35. *Inter:* Yes they sent me a check.

The same is observed in the wind-down phase of the OPI, as the following excerpts from various OPI wind-downs illustrate:

170. *Cand: Are you in Washington?*
171. *Inter:* Yes. Uh-huh.
172. *Cand: But I know that during the summer it's very hot at Washington also?*

173. *Inter:* Oh yes yes this summer we were we I think that we were we had the kind of weather you're used to down there . . in the summer.
174. *Cand:* Yes, oh yes almost the same
175. *Inter:* It was very much in the 100's days . . day after day after day in the in the high 90's and 100's it was just and and high humidity.
176. *Cand: It's funny I: why it's so hot during the summer. And during the winter [c] do you have snow sometime?*

This excerpt taken from tape 101 clearly illustrates a major departure from the level check and probes patterns. Here the candidate is allowed to ask questions and thus more actively participate in the new topic nomination so characteristic of conversation. The informal character of an interaction, with the candidate's greater involvement in the interaction, is also evident in the following excerpt from tape 201, in which the candidate invites the tester to go on a trip to Vietnam:

526. *Cand:* Don't forget Okay
527. *Inter:* Okay I've got your name I told you I've got your name so (laughs)
528. *Cand:* Just buy me a round-trip ticket and I'll [c] all the food.
529. *Inter:* What I see you come cheaply right?
530. *Cand:* Very I only.
531. *Inter:* Only a ticket. That's great.
532. *Cand:* Only a ticket.
534. *Inter:* And you'll feed me there.

535. *Cand:* Yes.

536. *Inter:* Okay We've we've we've got a deal right.

The DA study results indicate that the OPI speech event represents an interview of two types: a survey research interview and a sociolinguistic interview. It is *not* representative of real-life conversation as the ETS claims. These findings raise some questions as to people's perceptions of the OPI speech event. Will testers and nontesters perceive and judge the OPI as an interview, a conversation, or a classroom interaction? How will they perceive the warm-up phase and the wind-down phase? How will they perceive the level check and probes phases? Will testers, because of their training, have different perceptions of the OPI from nontesters? In the next chapter, I shall answer these questions triggered by the DA study findings.

# Chapter 6

## NATIVE SPEAKERS'
## PERCEPTIONS OF THE
## OPI SPEECH EVENT

In this chapter, I shall describe a semantic differential study that aims at investigating the nature of the OPI from the outside perspective. In the previous chapter, I presented evidence from the inside perspective. That is, based on a quantitative data analysis of thirty-five OPIs, I have identified the salient features of the OPI communicative speech event. Here, I shall investigate how testers and nontesters perceive what it is that has been done in the OPI, and whether testers and nontesters differ as to their perceptions or judgments of the OPI communicative speech event. Recall that according to Hymes (1974), the knowledge of structures and functions of speech events constitutes an integral part of native speakers' communicative competence. Therefore, if the findings of the discourse analysis are correct, the native speaker's perceptions should be consistent with the findings of the discourse analysis study.

## The Semantic Differential Instrument

In this study, the testers' and nontesters' perceptions/judgments of the OPI speech event are measured through a semantic differential instrument. Charles E. Osgood (1957) is considered the originator of the semantic differential (SD) instrument. The SD represents his attempt to measure meaning qualitatively.

In Osgood's SD instrument each concept is associated with a series of unidimensional scales that subjects are asked to evaluate. It is important to point out that these scales are not designed to tell what a concept is, but rather how the subject feels about a given concept, for example, war or Jerry. The scales measure the connotative rather than the denotative meaning of words. Some concepts that are denotatively different may be connotatively similar, that is, they both may evoke the same feeling.

Osgood provides detailed instructions as to how to construct SD instruments, how to select the variables that best capture the meaning of concepts, and how to write instructions. In the *Measurement of Meaning,* Osgood (1957) presents a list of the factors that have already been determined for certain groups of concepts. The application of the SD can vary. The SD can be used as a well-established, validated instrument to compare individual subjects' judgments of given concepts—to determine whether individual subjects change their attitudes toward the same concept over time—or to compare groups of subjects' judgment or attitude toward the same concepts. Precisely because its validity for comparing groups or individual subjects' judgments or attitudes is well established, the SD instrument has been used in language attitude and motivation research studies (Gardner and Lambert 1972). The established validity of the instrument, along with its usage in similar types of studies dealing with people's perceptions/judgments of language use, was the main reason for selecting this instrument to determine native speakers' perceptions of the OPI.

The following represents the SD form that was used in the SD data collection process:

*Semantic Differential:*
The purpose of this study is to get some idea of your impression of the recorded samples of the oral test. In particular, we would like to know how you feel about the sample(s) you will hear. You will see that on each line there are two words expressing opposites.
For example, under

*FORMAT*
A    B    C    D    E    F    G
Difficult ____:____:____:____:____:____:____ Easy

If you were to mark "A," it would mean that you think that the format of the just heard sample was *extremely* difficult. If you were to mark "G," it would mean that you think that the format was *extremely* easy. The central position

"D" indicates that you think that the format was *neutral*; that is, neither easy or difficult.

IMPORTANT: (1) Please place your check-marks in the middle of the space, not on the boundaries

(2) Please check all the items

(3) Please never put more than one check-mark.

Please go rapidly through all the items. It is your immediate impression in which we are interested.

PLEASE MARK YOUR ANSWERS
ON THE ANSWER SHEET.

### FORMAT

|   | A | B | C | D | E | F | G |   |
|---|---|---|---|---|---|---|---|---|
| 01. formal | __:__:__:__:__:__:__ | | | | | | | informal |
| 02. conversation-like | __:__:__:__:__:__:__ | | | | | | | interview-like |
| 03. natural | __:__:__:__:__:__:__ | | | | | | | contrived |
| 04. spontaneous | __:__:__:__:__:__:__ | | | | | | | controlled |

### TESTER

|   | A | B | C | D | E | F | G |   |
|---|---|---|---|---|---|---|---|---|
| 05. spontaneous | __:__:__:__:__:__:__ | | | | | | | controlled |
| 06. uncooperative | __:__:__:__:__:__:__ | | | | | | | cooperative |
| 07. active/involved | __:__:__:__:__:__:__ | | | | | | | passive/uninvolved |
| 08. formal | __:__:__:__:__:__:__ | | | | | | | informal |

### QUESTIONS

|   | A | B | C | D | E | F | G |   |
|---|---|---|---|---|---|---|---|---|
| 09. varied | __:__:__:__:__:__:__ | | | | | | | repetitive |
| 10. unnatural | __:__:__:__:__:__:__ | | | | | | | natural |

11. conversation-    __:__:__:__:__:__:__ interview-
    like                                         like
12. formal          __:__:__:__:__:__:__ informal

### CANDIDATE
A   B   C   D   E   F   G

13. tense           __:__:__:__:__:__:__ relaxed
14. formal          __:__:__:__:__:__:__ informal
15. active/involved __:__:__:__:__:__:__ passive/
                                             uninvolved
16. uncooperative   __:__:__:__:__:__:__ cooperative

### TOPIC NOMINATION
A   B   C   D   E   F   G

17. interview-      __:__:__:__:__:__:__ conversation-
    like                                         like
18. negotiated      __:__:__:__:__:__:__ controlled
19. repetitive      __:__:__:__:__:__:__ varied
20. formal          __:__:__:__:__:__:__ informal

### TURN TAKING
A   B   C   D   E   F   G

21. varied          __:__:__:__:__:__:__ fixed
22. controlled      __:__:__:__:__:__:__ uncontrolled
23. formal          __:__:__:__:__:__:__ informal
24. conversation-   __:__:__:__:__:__:__ interview-
    like                                         like

## Data Description

For the SD study eight participants were selected. Four of
them are OPI English testers at the Defense Language In-

stitute and the remaining four are "naive" native speakers of English. The selection of the eight participants was determined on the basis of several criteria, including age, education, and willingness to participate in the study. The participants were divided into two groups: testers and nontesters. Within each group there were two females and two males. The age of the participants ranged from thirty-five to fifty-five. All participants have a master's degree in the field either of TESL, education, or computer science. All have some background in studying foreign languages.

For the purpose of the SD study, sixteen OPIs—four OPIs per base level—were randomly selected from the pool of thirty-five transcribed and coded OPIs analyzed in chapter 5 of this book. The author, an OPI tester and tester trainer herself, selected the warm-up, level check and probes, and wind-down phases of the OPIs. All are representative samples of each phase of the OPI.

For each randomly selected OPI, the author prepared three SD forms—one for the warm-up, one for the level check and probes, one for the wind-down. The reason for conducting an SD for each individual phase of the OPI was to determine whether the specific phases of the OPI are perceived differently. That is, one speech event may be associated with the level check and probes phases of the OPI and a different one with the wind-down phase; for instance, the wind-down may be more conversation-like and the level check and probes more interview-like. Also, it may be the case that a level 4 level check and probes may exhibit different speech event characteristics than a level 2 level check and probes phase of the OPI.

It is important to note that when asked to listen to a portion of an OPI, the participants were not informed that they were listening to the warm-up or wind-down phase of the OPI. Some of the testers, however, recognized the phases of the OPI, saying, "Okay, now it is the wind-down." The author, who prepared the appropriate SD forms, marked the backs of the SD forms so as to be able later on to distinguish between various phases of a given OPI.

Collection of the SD data took approximately five weeks. The author met with the eight participants individually two and sometimes three times a week for an hour, with the exception of the first session, which lasted an hour and a half. Each of these individual sessions proceeded in the following manner. First, the participants were asked to read the introduction to the SD. Second, they listened to the selected portion of the OPI. Third, they filled out the SD form. Each participant listened to sixteen OPIs (four for each base level) and filled out fifty-six SD forms.

## Data Analysis of the Semantic Differential Study

The analysis of the SD data proceeded in three steps. However, before these three steps are described in detail, some explanation as to the terminology and the content of the

SD form is needed to assist in the interpretation of the SD data analysis results.

As stated earlier, the SD instrument used in the study consists of six categories: format, tester, question, candidate, topic nomination, and turn taking. For each major category, there are four scales. Thus, overall there are twenty-four scales on each SD form. Each scale includes a pair of opposing adjectives, such as "formal-informal," placed on a scale that ranges from 1 to 7.

In some instances, the sequence of the same adjectives has been reversed to prevent the repetition of the same pattern. Thus, if one major category included the pair of adjectives: "formal/informal," the order of the adjectives in the major category immediately following may have been reversed to read "informal/formal." The scales that include the same pairs of opposing adjectives reflect the same aspects (for example, the aspect of formality, naturalness, simplicity, cooperation, and so on). The scales that express the same aspect were aggregated in stages 2 and 3 of the SD data analysis. For instance, the SD form includes six scales expressing the aspect of formality: these are scales 01, 08, 12, 14, 20, and 23. In these instances the individual scales expressing the same aspects were aggregated, and a conversion procedure was performed. In the conversion process, a value of 1 was always assigned to adjectives that capture more rigid, formal, fixed, interview-like aspects of interaction; a value of 7 was assigned to adjectives that de-scribe/reflect more flexible, informal, conversation-like aspects of interaction. To illustrate this process let's take as an example the individual scales 02, 11, 17, and 24.

All but scale 24 read:

$$\begin{array}{ccccccc} 7 & 6 & 5 & 4 & 3 & 2 & 1 \\ A & B & C & D & E & F & G \end{array}$$

conversation-like __:__:__:__:__:__:__ interview-like

Scale 24 in the SD reads:

$$\begin{array}{ccccccc} 1 & 2 & 3 & 4 & 5 & 6 & 7 \\ A & B & C & D & E & F & G \end{array}$$

interview-like __:__:__:__:__:__:__ conversation-like

In this way "conversation-like" is always assigned a value of 7, and "interview-like" is always assigned a value of 1.

As indicated earlier, the SD data analysis proceeded in three stages, from the most global/broadest stage (stage 1) to the most detailed stage of analysis (stage 3).

In the *first* stage, the scales expressing the same aspect were aggregated for the entire OPI. For instance, the scales aimed at capturing the aspect of formality were combined across all three phases of the OPI. At stage 1 of the SD data analysis, the division among phases of the OPI was erased, and the comparison of the testers' and nontesters' impressions of the collapsed individual scales (expressing the same aspect) across all four levels of speaking proficiency was determined. A two-analysis of variance was performed within each stage. An analysis of variance statistical procedure was selected due to the fact that in this factorial design there are two independent variables: (a) Groups (that is, TESTER), with two levels, testers and nontesters; and (b) level of speaking proficiency with four levels: 1, 2, 3, 4. Where the ANOVA F ratio was significant, a Student-Newman-Keuls (SNK) post hoc statistical procedure was performed.

In the *second* stage, the individual scales expressing the same aspect within each phase of the OPI (that is, warm-up, level check and probes, and wind-down) were aggregated. An analysis of variance was performed, followed, where appropriate, by a post hoc statistical procedure (SNK).

In the *third* stage, an attempt was made to determine (that is, to compare) whether there was a significant difference between the testers' and nontesters' judgments of each individual scale across all four levels of speaking proficiency. That is, all individual scales within the six categories such as format, tester, topic, and so on were compared (that is, twenty-four scales within the warm-up phase, twenty-four scales within the level check and probes phase, and twenty-four within the wind-down phase across all four levels of speaking proficiency were compared). A two-way analysis of variance was performed, followed, where appropriate, by an SNK statistical procedure.

The SD data analysis consists of a large number of the ANOVA and Student-Newman-Keuls table results. Readers are encouraged to refer to Johnson (1997) for a detailed statistical analysis results of each stage. In this section, I shall summarize the SD data analysis results for stages 1, 2, and 3.

## Summary of the Results for Stage 1

The most global stage of the SD data analysis, stage 1, provides the least detailed information regarding the testers' and nontesters' perceptions/judgments of the OPI speech event. It offers the vaguest picture of the OPI in terms of their perceptions. The picture that emerges from this stage of analysis is that the OPI speech event, in the testers' and nontesters' judgments, is neither conversational in nature nor interview-like in nature; it is neither natural nor contrived; it is neither spontaneous nor controlled; it is neither formal nor informal; it is neither varied nor repetitive. Despite its vagueness, this stage offers, however, one very important piece of information: the OPI does not allow for much negotiation on the part of the candidate. Both testers and nontesters agree that the OPI as a whole is controlled in nature. Also, this broadest level of the SD analysis highlights the difference between level 3 and other levels, level 4 in particular.

## Summary of the Results for Stage 2

Stage 2 of the SD data analysis presents a rather uniform view of the OPI on the part of the testers and nontesters, especially in regard to the level check and probes phases. In contrast to the warm-up and the wind-down phases, the level check and probes are viewed by both testers and nontesters as formal, interview-like, controlled, and fixed. Both the warm-up and the wind-down are viewed by the SD participants as more conversation-like, less formal, more varied, and controlled, but less controlled than the level check and probes in the estimation of both groups. The groups differ somewhat as to the degree of some aspects of the warm-up. The testers view the warm-up as more conversation-like than the nontesters. They also view the warm-up as more informal, more natural, and more varied than the nontesters. The OPI training workshop may offer some explanation as to these differences between the testers and nontesters. The OPI testers are trained to view the warm-up as conversational, informal, casual, and spontaneous. The testers and nontesters expressed their favorable impression toward the participants in the OPI interaction, perceiving them as being active and cooperative.

The analysis of the wind-down draws our attention to level 3. Both testers and nontesters gave the least favorable evaluation of level 3 wind-down. In comparison to other wind-downs, level 3 wind-down is perceived by both groups as the least informal, spontaneous, and varied.

Because these two stages of the SD analysis are based on the combined aspects, many details regarding the testers' and nontesters' perceptions of the OPI and its phases were missing. In order to obtain detailed information regarding their perceptions of the OPI communicative speech event, stage 1 of the SD data analysis (that is, the analysis of individual scales) was performed.

## Summary of the SD Data Analysis Findings for Stage 3

The findings of stage 3 of the SD data analysis show that in the perception of the testers and nontesters, the level check and probes differ substantially from the other two phases. the warm-up phase and the wind-down phase. The testers and nontesters express their greatest overall uniformity as to their perception of the level check and probes phases. The format of the level check and probes is viewed by both testers and nontesters as formal, interview-like, and controlled. The topic nomination within the level check and probes is perceived by both groups as interview-like, very controlled, and formal. The turn-taking mechanism in the level check and probes is perceived by both testers and nontesters as controlled, formal, and interview-like. The participants in the two groups agree that the tester's verbal behavior within this phase is even less spontaneous and more formal than in the other phases.

The testers' and nontesters' judgments of the level check and probes seem to confirm the DA study findings. Both groups express their perception of the level check and probes as a very formal type of interview, formal in format, formal in the nature of question types, and controlled by the testers. Their perception seems to confirm the DA findings that this phase of the OPI represents a formal verbal exchange—a survey research interview.

The testers' and nontesters' perception of the warm-up and the wind-down differs from their perception of the level check and probes phases. In contrast to the level check and probes, the warm-up phase is perceived by both testers and nontesters as more conversation-like, more natural, more spontaneous, and varied in terms of the format, topic nomination, and question types. However, the testers judged this phase as being more conversation-like than nontesters. This should not be surprising since the OPI testers are trained to consider this phase very conversation-like in nature. What seems to be significant, however, is that both testers and nontesters perceive turn-taking distribution to be controlled, which points toward the kind of asymmetry of power typical of an interview in general. The testers' and nontesters' perception of this phase seems to support the DA findings (that is, the warm-up represents a different type of interview—a sociolinguistic interview).

The testers' and nontesters' perception of the wind-down phase is similar to their perception of the warm-up phase. The findings of the SD analysis show that in contrast to the level check and probes phases and similar to the warm-up phase both groups perceived this phase as being more conversation-like, more informal in terms of the format, question types, and topic nomination. However, the testers perceived the format of the wind-down as less natural and less spontaneous than the nontesters. Also, the testers perceived the questions posed within this phase as less informal than the nontesters. Again, the OPI testers training may offer some explanation as to this difference in perception between the testers and nontesters. The OPI testers are trained to view the wind-down phase as "the interviewer's last chance to check any aspect of the candidate's ability that may still be incompletely assessed" (ETS 1992: 24). For the "outsiders"—nontesters—the format and type of questioning may give an impression of being casual and spontaneous, but to the testers, the wind-down phase allows assessment of the candidate's speaking ability.

The SD data analysis also reveals that level 3 wind-down stands out in comparison to other level wind-downs, especially level 4 wind-down. In comparison to other levels, level 3 wind-down is viewed by both testers and non-testers as the least spontaneous in terms of the format, the least varied in terms of question types, and the least informal in terms of the pattern of topic nomination. The level 3 candidate is perceived as being the most tense and formal.

A careful analysis of the transcripts of all level 3 wind-downs used in the SD study has prompted the following observations that seem to provide some answers to the level 3 wind-down phenomenon. For example, in the OPI tape 303 wind-down, there is a very short preclosing:

> *155. Inter:* It was terrible. Well listen I tell you what I am going to let you go now and speak in Spanish for a while. Before I do I want to thank you very much for ask an answering all my questions so patiently
> *156. Cand:* My pleasure sir.
> *157. Inter:* And I want to wish you good luck in your Spanish conversation.
> *158. Cand:* All right thank you sir.
> *159. Inter:* Take care.
> *160. Cand:* My pleasure.
> *161. Inter:* Bye bye.
> *162. Cand:* Bye bye.

In the middle part of the wind-down phase tape 305, the tester tries to "clear unfinished facets" by introducing a supported opinion task: "Do you think that we should have uh uh telev trials televised as they're doing with the Simpson trial" that in style and content sounds very similar to the questions posed in the level check and probes phases. One gets the impression that the tester tries to reopen the level check phase:

179. *Inter:* Mm-hm well [c] I've enjoyed talking to you and I wish you a lot of good luck and not very many and no irate passengers in your (laughs) in your job. I imagine you're very busy right now with the vacation season.

180. *Cand:* Uh I'm not working right now I'm off for six weeks.

181. *Inter:* Oh I see!

182. *Cand:* I'll be going back in August fifteen I think it is.

183. *Inter:* Ah good well I hope you're taking it easy and and sitting around and listening to a lot of music and

184. *Cand:* From those OJ theme from the office. (laughs)

185. *Inter:* Oh (laughs)

186. *Cand:* I was doing it.

187. *Inter:* Well I think of course that's always very easy to get addicted to. *Do you think that we should have uh uh telev trials televised as they're doing with the Simpson trial?*

The wind-down phase of the OPI tape 306 sounds almost like the end of a formal job interview:

215. *Inter:* Well listen ma'am I am going to stick to my promise I have no further questions that I have on my my list that I wanted to ask you. What you and I will do now in just a couple moments we'll hang up and your contact person or your applicant coordinator there in Philadelphia will call back to our headquarters and you'll be speaking with an en-

tirely different person this time in Chinese. But now before I go I want to thank you for having been so cooperative with me it was a pleasure talking with you and wasn't any kind of task at all for me it was a very easy thing for me to do. I want to wish you much success on your Chinese conversation and to have a Merry Christmas.

216. *Cand:* Thank you very much
217. *Inter:* Thank you so much
218. *Cand:* Okay. Thank you
219. *Inter:* Take care now. Bye bye
220. *Cand:* Bye bye.

The wind-down of the OPI tape 308 ends abruptly:

197. *Inter:* So that's always the uh the other thing y'know. Uh nice talking to you.
198. *Cand:* Likewise
199. *Inter:* Uh and good luck to you.
200. *Cand:* Thank you.
201. *Inter:* O.K.
202. *Cand:* Mm-hm
203. *Inter:* See you again. Bye bye.

In contrast to level 3 wind-downs, level 4 wind-downs sound more conversation-like, more informal, and more natural. The following excerpt from the OPI tape 406 illustrates this difference:

134. *Cand:* Oh I know I know it's uh I I've I did go to Europe many times but I never I've never gone to Spain and a lot of people have asked me if I've been there and that's one thing I need to I need to do but

uh if I do go I I don't want to go for maybe a week or two I think it needs to be a lot longer than that.

*135. Inter:* Well at least dancing-wise you'll be ready so (laughs)

*136. Cand:* Well I hope. (laughs)

*137. Inter:* Well I've enjoyed talking to you and I I wish you the very best I I see you're applying as a contract linguist?

*138. Cand:* Yes.

*139. Inter:* And are you looking for another full-time job at the same time or are you ?

*140. Cand:* No I don't have a job right now.

*141. Inter:* Well the advantage of being a contract person is that you can more or less it's it's very flexible

*142. Cand:* Uh-huh.

*143. Inter:* Advantage to working in that type of [c] but I wish you the best of luck and I've enjoyed talking to you.

*144. Cand:* O.K. yeah I've enjoyed talking to you also.

*145. Inter:* Bye bye.

*146. Cand:* Bye bye.

The overall impression is that the testers who conducted level 3 OPIs need some improvement in the area of elicitation techniques pertaining to the wind-down phase of the OPI.

The findings of the SD study support the DA study findings reported in chapter 5. They confirm that the OPI does not test speaking ability in "a real-life context—conversation" (ETS 1982: 13). The OPI tests speaking ability in the form of a unique type of interview, which I shall describe and discuss in the next chapter.

# CHAPTER 7

# A PROTOTYPICAL MODEL
# OF THE
# OPI COMMUNICATIVE
# SPEECH EVENT

The DA study findings provide empirical evidence as to the communicative nature of the OPI's speech event. That is, they answer the question, What kind of speech event is the OPI? is it more like an everyday conversation, an interview, or a classroom interaction? The OPI speech event is like *an interview*. More precisely, the OPI represents a unique type of interview that is closely associated with a given phase of the OPI. That is, the level check and probes phases represent *a survey research interview,* and the warm-up and wind-down represent *a sociolinguistic interview.*

The findings of the SD study provide empirical evidence for the question, Do native speakers (testers versus nontesters) differ in their judgments of the nature of the

OPI communicative speech event? With a few exceptions where testers and nontesters differ as to the *degree* of certain aspects within the warm-up and wind-down phases of the OPI, testers and nontesters do *not* differ in their overall judgments of the nature of the OPI communicative speech event. Their judgments as to the level check and probes phases of the OPI are completely uniform. Testers' and nontesters' perceptions of the level check and probes phases of the OPI and the warm-up and wind-down phase support the DA empirical findings. The level check and probes phases differ in both testers' and nontesters' judgments from the warm-up and wind-down phases; the former represents a very formal type of interview—a survey research interview—and the latter represents a more conversation-like type of interview—a sociolinguistic interview.

The combined empirical findings of the DA and the SD have led to the development of a prototypical model of the OPI communicative speech event (figure 7.1).

## Theoretical and Practical Implications of the DA and SD Findings

In chapter 1, I stated that the main purpose of this book is to provide some answers to two questions, the first of which is, Is the Oral Proficiency Interview (OPI) a valid instrument for assessing language speaking proficiency? Recall that the Educational Testing Service (1982: 13) claims that "a well-structured oral proficiency interview tests speak-

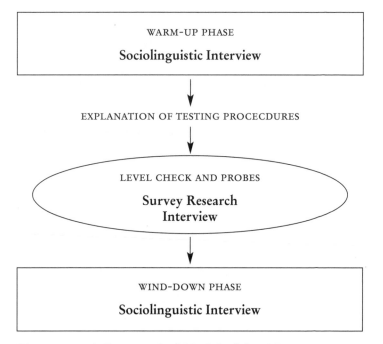

Figure 7.1    A Prototypical Model of the OPI
             Communicative Speech Event

ing ability in a real-life context—a conversation. It is almost by definition a valid measure of speaking ability."

The empirical findings presented in chapters 5 and 6 contradict the ETS's claim. The OPI does *not* test speaking ability in the real-life context of a conversation. The OPI tests speaking ability in the context of an interview, and, to be more precise, in the context of two types of interviews, sociolinguistic and survey research. This raises the question of the validity of the OPI testing instrument.

Recall that the OPI's proponents consider its content validity as proof of the test's validity. Messick (1989: 17), however, points out that establishing content validity of language performance tests is not enough:
"In a fundamental sense so-called content validity does not count as validity at all . . . Some test specialists contend that what a test is measuring is operationally defined by specifying the universe of item content and the item-selection process. But as we shall see, determining what a test is measuring always requires recourse to other form of evidence." This other form of evidence is construct validity, which Messick (1989: 13) defines as "An integrated evaluative judgment of the degree to which empirical evidence and theoretical rationales support the adequacy and appropriateness of inferences and actions based on test scores." In the context of this definition, the OPI lacks both the empirical evidence and theoretical rationales to justify the claim about the conversational nature of its interaction.

From the social consequences point of view, the findings warn against spreading false information about the nature of the OPI speech event. Such a misinterpretation can have a profound impact on the OPI users' ability to generalize the candidate's ability based on his/her test score to the outside world. For example, since the OPI claims to be conversational in nature, the users of the test may be under the impression that the candidate who obtained a level 2 or higher rating is able to fully participate in a conversation. That is, the candidate is able to compete for the floor, negotiate a new topic, and so forth. The findings of the DA and SD studies show that the candidate does not have many opportunities to prove the mastery of these skills. The phases in which the candidate may exhibit more initiative—the warm-up and the wind-down—are minimized in the process of assigning a global rating. The final rating is based on the candidate's performance within the level check and probes—the phases wherein the candidate's power to negotiate is almost nonexistent.

To improve this situation, the OPI training programs should include samples of natural conversations, so that the OPI testers could be reminded about typical characteristics of everyday conversation. Testers need to be aware of the fact that preclosings, for instance, constitute a natural part of everyday conversation. Improvement is also urgently needed regarding the so-called lead-in questions (that is, questions that lead to a given task), especially within the level check and probes phases. Improvement in this area might alleviate the impression that testers are working from a prescribed set of questions based on their current reading of political and economic news. Testers should also be encouraged to avoid making any evaluative remarks such as, "Very good, let's move to the next question." "Very good. We made it." "Good, very good." "Okay. I have asked you all the questions from my list." They also should be encouraged to avoid making the fol-

tant moment for the testers in their process of assessing the candidate's speaking proficiency level. The format indicates that the tester is probing the candidate by asking her to perform a level 3 task (that is, a supported opinion question). The candidate's responses are taken as evidence that she does not have the linguistic ability to perform at that level. Therefore, she is given a level 2 rating. One may wonder, however, what might have happened if the testers had allowed the candidate to negotiate topic; if they had changed the topic to one in which the candidate showed some expertise and interests, namely, the topic of nursing.

The same phenomenon is evident in my current data. Despite candidates' clear signals of discomfort regarding the topic nominated by the tester, candidates are forced to continue to express their opinions. For example, in the following excerpt, the candidate, a refugee from Iraq, is asked to express his opinion about the political situation in Iraq, specifically about Saddam Hussein. The candidate's tone of voice and his frequent hesitations and pauses (turns 114, 116) clearly indicate that he does not feel comfortable discussing this topic. The candidate seems to be afraid to express his opinions on that topic. Perhaps he is afraid because he still has family members living in Iraq. Recall that the whole interaction is being recorded, and the OPI is being conducted by an official government agency in Washington, D.C. From his evasive responses and his upset tone of voice, it is difficult to determine whether he does not have the required language ability to perform a level 3 task or if he is simply afraid to express his opinion and his nervousness affects his performance (tape 208):

> *113. Inter:* Since you lived in Iraq, I would be interested in knowing .. what your .. what your observations were as far as that country's government is concerned. Do you see any possibility that perhaps Saddam Hussein will not be in power much longer .. he might loose his grip on on political structure, or do you think that he is going to be there for the foreseeable future?
>
> *114. Cand:* Uh .. you know honestly .. *I really don't know* .. I mean .. what is going to happen. Certainly now the status in Iraq is very bad *uh uh*. You know .. this is what I hear .. and .. if the .. the people are given chance to .. to voice their opinion, then he *uh uh* wouldn't be in power very long. You know *uh uh uh* .. but then it depends how .. hard he is on people you know because .. he really doesn't give people the freedom of speech or .. to say something .. you know so .. it's very difficult to predict what .. what .. he .. he will do *uh uh*. He has been in power for so many years and he has done it by being there .. and by .. it's like *uh uh uh* dictatorship thing .. you know .. *uh uh* and so .. who knows what .. what he is going to do.
>
> *115. Inter:* You see, the reason I asked the question=
> *Cand:* ⌈sure      ⌉
> *Inter:* ⌊it seem⌋ed to me when you were describing your own past and bit about Iraq it seemed .. and the question arose in my mind .. well if this coun-

try is so diverse, there is certainly a different kinds
of groups and so many different interests, you have
Christians, you have Arabs, you have Kurds, you
have this group that group, how is this man able to
keep hold of all this people without . . you know of
some kind of dissent arising.

*116. Cand:* Oh I mean he . . he likes he holds every-
body . . and nobody dares to say anything to him,
you know, they can't express their opinion and
and . . it's like *fear*, you know, *uh uh* this is what is
happening there. And nobody can say anything *uh
uh uh* that's why he can do . . *uh uh uh* they can't
speak up uh they can't tell what's ailing them . . he
will just dominate the whole thing uh, I mean *uh uh*
when . . has bad repercussions on the economy of
the country like . . you know when the United Na-
tions impose sanctions, sanctions against Iraq uh
that was very bad for the people uh because people
probably, they have nothing to with that . . right,
you know . . *uh uh* that was his decision . . and . .
that would be bad for the country.

*117. Inter:* Well, I suppose one can make the same case
for Haiti in that regard, for Cuba in that regard and
every country we deal with we do with that. Any
kind of the embargo always tends to

*Cand:* ⌐yeah⌐

*Inter:* ⌊like ⌋ but in the case of Cuba when we put . .
we had an embargo, the Cubans in the United
States said, no, no, don't take it off, leave the pressure on, otherwise nothing will happen, that was a
similar kind of situation of Iraq, that that Iraqi-
American feel that we should, should put more

pressure on or they tend to say, no, no, take it off, you are hurting the people.

*118. Cand:* See .. *really really I don't have .. I am not I am not in touch with any Iraqi people=*

*Inter:* Uh-huh

*Cand:* =you know, and .. I haven't spoken to any of them.

*119. Inter:* So, you can't speak for the community as a whole.

*120. Cand:* Yes, uh, I don't.

In this example, the tester selects the topic of a political situation to elicit a level 3 task—a supported opinion task. Since the candidate has received a level 2 rating, in the tester's opinion, the candidate must have failed to perform the selected level 3 task. One may wonder, however, what might have happened if the selected topic had been less emotional and sensitive to the candidate, if the candidate's performance would have been different, if he had been allowed to talk on a topic of his interest.

The tester's increased awareness about the effects of topic nomination on the candidate's performance would not only improve the OPI's reliability but its validity as well. Recall that within the current view of validity, reliability can be regarded as one type of evidence for validity; therefore, by improving the consistency (that is, reliability) with which the tester elicits language samples during the OPI, the validity of the OPI could be enhanced as well.

Furthermore, the existence of two types of interviews, a survey and a sociolinguistic interview, within the OPI may be very confusing to the candidate. The abrupt change from the warm-up phase, in which the candidate is given greater control over what is talked about and in which the tester expresses some involvement in the interaction, to a very formal level check may send an unexpected signal to the candidate that he/she could have done something wrong. How else can one explain this abrupt change in the tester's behavior from a friendly and engaged participant to an emotionless evaluator of the candidate's responses?

The existence of the two speech events within the OPI creates an entirely new speech event that does not correspond to any speech event in real life. Therefore, candidates cannot use their real-world knowledge about the rules of speaking to guide them during the OPI. Candidates cannot rely on their knowledge of the rules of speaking in conversation because as soon as they get a sense that this could indeed be a friendly conversation with a stranger, the rules of speaking change drastically. This abrupt change from one speech event to another may affect candidates' emotional state, which, in turn, may affect their verbal performance.

Except during a police interrogation, in real life it is highly unlikely to encounter an exchange between two strangers in which only one person has a right to ask many unrelated and often insensitive questions, and the other person has an obligation to provide a full response to each question. In a real-life situation, a person would be totally mystified by this type of questioning, not to mention that she/he would most likely decline to respond or participate in such an interaction.

In conclusion, let me point out that the purpose of the studies reported in chapters 5 and 6 was not to advocate the superiority or appropriateness of one form of speech event over the other. The purpose of these studies was to find out what the OPI measures. The findings contradict the claim as to the nature of the OPI communicative speech event and raise an important theoretical question: What is speaking ability? speaking ability that exists independently of testing instruments? In the next two chapters, I shall offer some theoretical and practical answers to this question.

# Chapter 8

# COMMUNICATIVE
# COMPETENCE VERSUS
# INTERACTIONAL
# COMPETENCE

Communicative competence represents a prevailing theoretical framework for second/foreign language teaching and testing. It has been popularized in second language teaching by the communicative language teaching approach (Richards and Rodgers 1986) and in language testing by the Test of English as a Foreign Language (TOEFL), which claims to measure students' communicative competence in English as a foreign language. Precisely because of its impact on second language teaching and testing, I shall provide a historical overview of the notion of communicative competence, and I shall describe the two most popular and influential models of communicative competence in second language theory and testing. I also address the controversy that currently exists regarding "proficiency" versus "communicative competence." That is, do these terms mean the same thing or do they represent different theoretical frameworks? The theoretical and practical effects of this state of confusion as to the meanings of these terms will be illustrated by the Test of Spoken English (TSE) and the Speaking Proficiency English Assessment Kit (SPEAK) test. At the end of the chapter, I shall describe the interactional competence model (Young 1999), which represents an alternative framework to communicative competence.

## A Historical Overview

In 1965, Chomsky wrote, "Linguistic theory is concerned primarily with an ideal speaker-listener, in a completely homogenous speech community, who knows its language perfectly and is unaffected by such grammatically irrelevant conditions as memory limitations, distractions, shifts of attention and interest, and errors (random or characteristic) in applying his knowledge of the language in actual performance" (Chomsky 1965: 3).

Chomsky divides linguistic theory into two parts: linguistic competence and linguistic performance. *Linguistic competence* concerns the tacit knowledge of grammar, and *linguistic performance* concerns the realization of this knowledge in actual performance. Chomsky's linguistic competence and performance can be traced back to de Saussure's (1959) structural linguistics. Chomsky's linguistic competence corresponds to the Saussurian *la langue* (a system of signs), and Chomsky's linguistic performance corresponds to the Saussurian *la parole* (the realization of this system in a particular situation). Chomsky's linguistic competence is viewed as superior to de Saussure's *la langue* because it is concerned primarily with underlying competences, and it advocates the speaker's ability to create or generate an unlimited number of grammatical sentences.

Chomsky is considered to be the originator of the notion of linguistic competence, which he associates with an ideal speaker's tacit knowledge of the grammatical structures of his/her native language. The ultimate goal of linguistic theory is to account for such grammatical knowledge. Chomsky distinctly relegates linguistic performance to the peripherals of linguistic inquiry. Linguistic performance as the actual use of language in concrete situations is viewed as "fairly degenerate in quality" (Chomsky 1965: 31) because performance is full of errors.

## Hymes's Communicative Competence Model

Hymes (1972) objected to Chomsky's definition of linguistic competence. He introduced the term *communicative competence* to expand Chomsky's definition of competence beyond the knowledge of tacit grammatical rules.

Hymes (1972: 278) stated that "there are rules of use without which the rules of grammar would be useless." According to Hymes, when a child acquires his/her native language, he/she acquires "knowledge of sentences, not only as grammatical, but appropriate. He or she acquires competence as to when to speak, when not, and as to what to talk about with whom, when, where and in what manner" (Hymes 1972: 277). He calls this competence to use the grammatical rules that are appropriate to a given social context *sociolinguistic competence*. Sociolinguistic competence undermines Chomsky's notion of a completely homogenous speech community by emphasizing the existence of a heterogeneous speech community devoid of an ideal speaker-listener.

Hymes also undermined Chomsky's definition of performance. He saw a flaw in it because of its inability to distinguish between performance as

1. (underlying) competence v. (actual) performance;
2. (underlying) grammatical competence v. (underlying) models/rules of performance. (Hymes 1972: 280)

That is, according to Hymes, Chomsky is not clear whether his performance should be viewed as "the actual use of language in concrete situations" (Chomsky 1965: 4) or as the underlying models/rules (that is, states or abilities) of performance not yet realized in the actual performance. Hymes (1972) calls these underlying modes/rules of performance *ability for use,* and he places "ability for use" within his new model of communicative competence. Thus, Hymes's communicative competence is "dependent upon both (tacit) knowledge and (ability) for use" (Hymes 1972: 282). For Hymes, this tacit knowledge includes both grammatical competence and sociolinguistic competence, and "ability for use," which he defines as "noncognitive factors, such as motivation" and other factors such as those identified by Goffman (1967): "Courage, gameness, gallantry, composure, presence of mind, dignity, stage confidence, capacities" (Hymes 1972: 283).

To summarize, Hymes's communicative competence model consists of two areas of competence: grammatical competence and sociolinguistic competence, and "ability for use." Communicative competence is separated from the actual performance in real-time, concrete situations. Hymes's communicative competence model can be illustrated as in figure 8.1.

## Canale and Swain's Communicative Competence Model

Hymes's model of first language communicative competence influenced the Canale and Swain 1980 model of second language communicative competence. The Canale and Swain model of communicative competence had a great impact on the field of second language teaching and testing

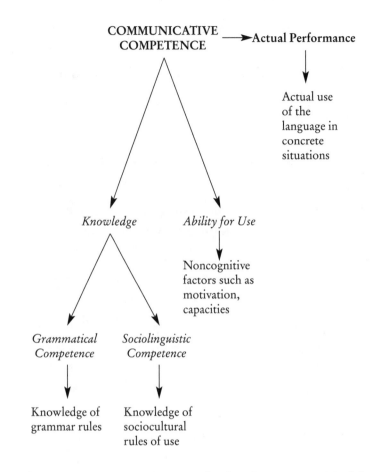

Figure 8.1     Hymes's Communicative Competence Model

for almost a decade. The Canale and Swain model originally consisted of three competencies: grammatical competence, sociolinguistic competence, and strategic competence. Later, the fourth competence, discourse competence, was added (Canale 1983). In their original 1980 model, discourse competence was considered to be a part of sociolinguistic competence.

*Grammatical competence* includes "the knowledge of lexical items and rules of morphology, syntax, sentence-grammar semantics and phonology" (1980: 29). *Sociolinguistic competence,* which is similar to Hymes's sociolinguistic competence, refers to the knowledge of sociocultural rules of use. *Strategic competence* is made up "of verbal and non-verbal communication strategies that may be called into action to compensate for breakdowns in communication due to performance variables, or to insufficient competence" (1980: 30). *Discourse competence* pertains to the knowledge of how to achieve cohesion and coherence in a text.

Unlike Hymes's model of communicative competence, the Canale and Swain (1980) model excludes ability for use (see McNamara 1996 for relevant discussion). Canale and Swain (1980: 7) provide the following reasons to justify their reluctance to incorporate the notion of ability for use in their communicative competence model: "(i) to our knowledge this notion has not been pursued rigorously in any research on communicative competence (or considered directly relevant in such research), and (ii) we doubt that there is any theory of human action that can adequately explicate 'ability for use' and support principles of syllabus design intended to reflect this notion." As McNamara (1996) points out, Canale and Swain recognize the complexity and difficulty associated with a broad list of the underlying rules of performance and refuse to open what McNamara calls a Pandora's box.

Contrary to Hymes, Canale and Swain (1980: 6) place ability for use in what they call communicative performance, which they define as "the realization of these competences [that is, their grammatical, sociolinguistic, strategic, and discourse competencies] and their interaction in the actual production and comprehension." The Canale and Swain 1980 model of communicative competence can be illustrated as in figure 8.2.

Despite Canale and Swain's efforts not to include Hymes's ability for use within their model of communicative competence, at least two of their competencies, strategic and discourse, include some elements of ability for use. It is difficult to imagine that nonverbal strategies, for example, represent only an individual's knowledge and not skills. The same reservation can apply to the notion of co-

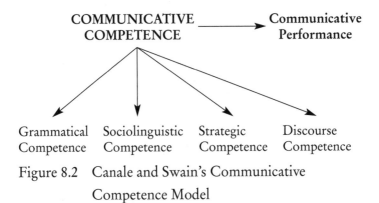

Figure 8.2    Canale and Swain's Communicative
            Competence Model

herence. It is difficult to imagine that the ability to create coherence in a text is only a matter of knowledge and not of skills or ability. Thus, despite their explicit refusal to open the Pandora's box, Canale and Swain implicitly introduce ability for use into their communicative model. Later on, Canale (1983) tries alone to correct this problem by including ability for use defined as "skills" within his revised model of communicative competence.

In addition to the problem of ability for use, there are some other problems with the Canale and Swain 1980 model. For example, although they claim that communicative competence requires interaction among four competencies in the actual production and comprehension, Canale and Swain do not provide any explanations as to how this interaction is to be achieved. That is, the mechanism responsible for the interaction among the four competences is not described and explained; only the outcome of this "unidentified" mechanism—interaction—is presented. Moreover, based on their definition of communicative competence, it is difficult to determine whether each of these four competences *equally* contributes to all the outcomes of interaction or whether each competence's contribution to interaction differs depending on the context of interaction.

There is also some ambiguity in their notion of interaction. That is, based on their definition, it is difficult to determine whether interaction takes place solely within the mind of the individual or outside the individual or both. For example, the use of strategic competence may be called into action as a result of other participants' lack of comprehension of the speaker's message, and the successful implementation of strategic competence may be accomplished only through other participants' collaboration or assistance.

As mentioned earlier, the Canale and Swain model, despite its shortcomings and lack of solid empirical evidence as to its validity, dominated the fields of second language teaching and testing for almost a decade. It was accepted as the main theoretical model for language teaching and language testing, and it remained unchallenged until Bachman (1990) introduced his communicative language ability (CLA) model.

## Bachman's Communicative Language Ability (CLA) Model

Bachman (1990: 84) describes CLA as "consisting of both knowledge or competence, and the capacity for implementing, or executing that competence in appropriate communicative language use." Bachman's model, which is based on the Canale and Swain model, consists of three competences: language competence, strategic competence, and psychophysiological mechanism. Of these three, the most important is strategic competence, which drastically differs from the Canale and Swain strategic competence. Recall that in the Canale and Swain model, strategic competence is defined as some sort of coping mechanism for the breakdown in communication. In contrast, Bachman's strategic competence pertains to general underlying cognitive skills in language use like assessing, planning, and executing, which are instrumental for achieving communicative goals. In Bachman's CLA model, strategic competence is separated from language competence. By separating language competence from strategic competence and by assigning nonlinguistic, cognitive underlying functions/rules to strategic competence, Bachman acknowledges the importance of including Hymes's ability for use in communicative competence models.

Furthermore, the importance of Bachman's strategic competence is also reinforced by its assigned function. The main function of Bachman's strategic competence is to relate language competence to the language user's knowledge of the world and to the features of the context in which language use takes place. Bachman's strategic competence represents a mechanism responsible for interaction, which, as previously mentioned, the Canale and Swain model lacks. That is, Bachman identifies and describes the mechanism that is responsible for producing the interaction among various components of his model. This function of strategic competence can be illustrated as in figure 8.3.

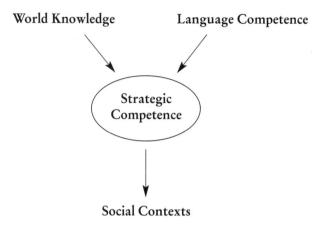

Figure 8.3    Bachman's CLA Model (adapted from Bachman 1990: 85)

Another important component of CLA, language competence, is divided into two major components: organizational competence and pragmatic competence. *Organizational competence* consists of two subcomponents: *grammatical competence*, defined as the knowledge of vocabulary, morphology, syntax, and phonology; and *textual competence*, defined as the knowledge of conventions of rhetorical organization and cohesion.

The second major component of language competence, *pragmatic competence*, is also divided into two subcomponents: illocutionary competence and sociolinguistic competence. *Illocutionary competence* is essential for the expression of a wide range of such language functions as ideational, manipulative, regulatory, interactional, heuristic, and imaginative functions; and *sociolinguistic competence* is defined as "the sensitivity to, or control of the conventions of language use" (1990: 94). Bachman (1990: 95) further defines the ability under sociolinguistic competence as "sensitivity to differences in dialect or variety, to differences in register and naturalness, and ability to interpret cultural references and figures of speech." Bachman's main components of language competence can be illustrated as in figure 8.4.

Although Bachman's CLA is regarded as an improved and expanded version of the Canale and Swain model, there are still some problems with it. For example,

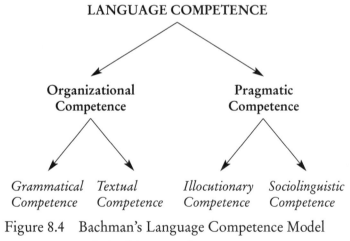

**LANGUAGE COMPETENCE**

**Organizational
Competence**

**Pragmatic
Competence**

*Grammatical
Competence*  *Textual
Competence*    *Illocutionary
Competence*  *Sociolinguistic
Competence*

Figure 8.4    Bachman's Language Competence Model
(adapted from Bachman 1990: 87)

like the Canale and Swain model, Bachman's presents a cognitive view of interaction. That is, in the CLA model, an individual is solely responsible for interaction. Also, Bachman presents a static view of interaction. This static view of interaction may be explained by Bachman's notion of social context, which he essentially defines a priori in terms of stable features of context like register, dialect, and variety. Social context is viewed as being autonomous and separated from other components. The possibility that language can create social context and social context can create language during actual interaction is not addressed in Bachman's model.

Furthermore, language competence divided into many different subcomponents gives an impression of being rather abstract and technical. Although one may argue that Bachman's subcomponents can be justified on logical grounds (McNamara 1996), they may be difficult to justify on practical and psychometric grounds. For instance, in his model, Bachman separates cohesion from coherence. He places cohesion under organizational, or textual, competence and moves coherence to pragmatic, or illocutionary, competence. From a logical point of view, this separation makes sense—indeed, cohesive devices represent linguistic signals for making connections between sentences or utterances—but from a practical point of view such a separation is difficult to implement.

CLA assumes that language ability represents not a unitary trait, but a multidimensional trait, and therefore that language ability can be measured not by one scale, but by a series of scales that measure each component of language ability separately. If this principle were to be applied to the Bachman language competence model, then one could get a very low score on cohesion and a very high score on coherence, and vice versa. The inferences based on this type of score would be difficult to generalize to real-life contexts. In real life, it is often difficult to separate cohesion and coherence because they are in a reciprocal relationship, and they are context dependent. That is, it is possible and appropriate to create a coherent text without using any explicit cohesive devices, as this now-famous exchange illustrates (Widdowson 1978: 29):

A: That's the telephone.
B: I am in the bath.
A: Okay.

Another problem with Bachman's language competence is that its definition of illocutionary competence is based on two theories: speech act theory (Austin 1962; Searle 1969) and language functions theory (Halliday 1973; Jakobson 1972). Combining these two theories within illocutionary competence is very confusing and inappropriate from a theoretical point of view because these two theories represent different theoretical backgrounds and methodologies. They also differ as to their view of context, which is essential for our ability to interpret the intended meaning of the speaker's utterances (Goodwin and Duranti 1972). The word *illocutionary* is associated with Searle's illocutionary acts, which he places at the core of human communication. He writes, "The basic unit of linguistic communication is the illocutionary act" (Searle 1969: 1). Such illocutionary acts as promising, requesting, and commanding are rule-governed, and their function is to communicate the speaker's intention toward the hearer. The effect of illocutionary acts on the hearer's actions and thoughts is called the prelocutionary act. The focus in speech act theory, however, is primarily on illocutionary acts of utterances—that is, on the communicative intentions of the speaker's utterances—and the ultimate goal of speech act theory is to identify and categorize all speech acts that are essential for the way people communicate in their everyday lives. This categorization is possible because people share rules that allow them to identify or label utterances as particular types of acts. These rules are part of people's linguistic competence, and they are closely associated with the features of contexts in which utterances are embedded. Thus, for example, an utterance can be labeled as "appointing" only if the person who does the appointing possesses the authority to do that.

Since speech act theory is very well established in the fields of pragmatics (Levinson 1983) and discourse analysis (Schiffrin 1994), it seems reasonable to ask researchers working in the fields of second language teaching and testing to either use these terms in their original forms or not to use them at all.

As mentioned earlier, in addition to Searle's speech act theory, Bachman's illocutionary competence includes such language functions as a heuristic function, which is the "use of language to extend our knowledge of the world" (Bachman 1990: 92), and a manipulative function, whose purpose is to affect, or manipulate, the world. It seems that the rationale for fusing these two theories is based on the presence of the word *function.* The notion of function, however, is used differently in the two theories. Speech act theory identifies everyday types of language functions, and language functions theory views functions in terms of broad philosophical purposes of human language.

If this fusion of the two understandings of the term *function* (that is, one everyday type of understanding and the other more abstract) were to be sustained, then there is a need to elaborate on their relationship. Are they independent of each other? or are they interrelated? And if interrelated, how so? The answers to these questions are important for the development of appropriate tasks that allow testers to elicit language functions and also for the development of scales that could appropriately evaluate the language learner's illocutionary competence.

There is also a problem with Bachman's definition of sociolinguistic competence. Recall that Bachman (1990: 94) defines sociolinguistic competence as "the sensitivity to or control of the conventions of language use," and he goes on to identify the abilities under sociolinguistic competence as "sensitivity to differences in dialect or variety, sensitivity to differences in register and naturalness, and the ability to interpret cultural references and figures of speech." Although Bachman's effort to identify these specific abilities under sociolinguistic competence is commendable, it is not clear whether his notion of sensitivity and control should fall under the category of language competence. Sensitivity, after all, can be viewed as a personality trait, as a person's ability to feel empathy, and not as language knowledge. It seems that Bachman's definition of sociolinguistic competence mixes the underlying rules/ models of performance (which is to say, Hymes's ability for use) with underlying language competence.

Neither Bachman's 1990 communicative language ability model nor the Canale and Swain 1980 communicative competence model has been empirically validated, although Bachman and Palmer (1982) found some empirical evidence for their distinction between pragmatic, grammatical, and sociolinguistic competences (Bachman 1990). The lack of empirical evidence as to these models' validity, abstractness, and theoretical complexity and the lack of clear definitions of what communicative competence is have contributed to the state of confusion that currently exists within the field of second language regarding the terms *communicative competence* and *proficiency.* Savignon (1983: 246) states that "language proficiency is communicative competence and should be defined and evaluated as such." Lantolf and Frawley (1985) see proficiency as separate from communicative competence, and they regard proficiency as devoid of any theoretical foundation other than proficiency testing: "Proficiency is what proficiency tests measure" (Lantolf and Frawley 1988: 185).

## Communicative Competence versus Proficiency

This confusion as to the proper meaning of the terms *communicative competence* versus *proficiency,* which unfortunately are often used interchangeably, has serious theoretical and practical consequences. To illustrate this point, I shall examine the design of two popular tests that are used to assess the speaking ability of international teaching assistants (ITAs) and of international students and international professionals who are nonnative speakers of English: the Test of Spoken English (TSE) and the Speaking Proficiency English Assessment Kit (SPEAK). These tests, which are sponsored by the ETS, are similar in content and purpose and are delivered in a semidirect format. That is, the format of the tests imitates a face-to-face interview. In both tests, the candidate is asked to respond to questions prerecorded on the audio tape. The SPEAK test is considered a nonsecure Test of Spoken English and, in contrast to the TSE, may be administered to examinees by institutions other than the ETS.

The SPEAK test consists of twelve questions/tasks, and the time allotted for each response ranges from thirty to ninety seconds. The candidate's performance on each question is rated holistically by two raters. The raters assign each of the twelve-item responses an individual holistic score on a scale that ranges from 20 to 60. The twelve items' scores are averaged, and the scores are reported in increments of 5, that is, 20, 25, 30, 35 up to 60. The overall scale consists of five levels:

> Level 20    No effective communication: no evidence of ability to perform
>
> Level 30    Communication generally effective: task performed poorly
>
> Level 40    Communication somewhat effective: task performed somewhat competently
>
> Level 50    Communication generally effective: task performed competently
>
> Level 60    Communication almost always effective: task performed very competently.
>
> (Educational Testing Service 1996)

In 1994, the theoretical construct of the TSE/ SPEAK test was revised to adhere to current approaches in second language theory and testing. Both tests now claim to measure communicative language ability, which includes two major components: language competence and strategic competence. *Language competence* consists of four competencies: functional, sociolinguistic, discourse, and linguistic competence. *Strategic competence* combines the Bachman and the Canale and Swain definitions of strategic competence. Like Bachman's strategic competence, the TSE/SPEAK strategic competence is separated from language competence, and it is partly defined as Bachman's strategic competence in terms of assessment, planning, assessing, and execution, and partly as Canale and Swain's sociolinguistic competence in terms of a coping mechanism for breakdowns in communication: "Strategic competence refers to the speaker's ability to assess the communicative situation, plan what to say, and execute the speech. Strategic competence also involves an ability to compensate for gaps in language ability by preventing or repairing communication breakdowns" (ETS 1996: 10).

*Functional competence,* defined as the speaker's ability to perform different language functions, closely resembles the functions included in the ILR/ETS/ACTFL scale descriptions: narration, directions, supported opinions, and persuasion. In fact, examination of the TSE/ SPEAK tests reveals that the functions and the format of the

TSE/SPEAK tests are modeled on the OPI tape-mediated test, which claims to represent *not* a communicative competence test, but a proficiency test (Lowe 1983).

Unlike the Bachman CLA model, the TSE/SPEAK model contains *discourse competence,* which is modeled on the Canale and Swain discourse competence and refers to the speaker's ability to organize the spoken information in a coherent and cohesive manner. The TSE/SPEAK *sociolinguistic competence,* with its focus on the speaker's sensitivity to sociolinguistic contexts, seems to adhere more to Bachman's sociolinguistic competence definition than to Canale and Swain's.

The TSE/SPEAK final component—linguistic competence, which refers to the speaker's knowledge of vocabulary morphology, syntax, and phonology—is similar to both Bachman's and Canale and Swain's grammatical competence.

To summarize, the TSE/SPEAK communicative language ability comprises within its design some elements of communicative competence based on the Canale and Swain model and the Bachman communicative language ability model, and some elements of proficiency based on the ILR skill level descriptions.

The TSE/SPEAK final rating—one global rating—indicates that the developers of the TSE/SPEAK tests do not seem to see any contradiction in combining some principles of proficiency theory with communicative competence theory. Recall that the ILR/ETS/ACTFL rating scales view proficiency as a unitary concept, whereas Bachman views communicative language ability as a nonunitary concept, one that can be expressed only in a series of ratings, not in a single rating. It would be interesting to learn how the TSE/SPEAK tests reconcile the multicomponentional nature of their communicative language ability with one holistic rating.

It seems that the TSE/SPEAK has benefited from the current controversy regarding the terms *proficiency* versus *communicative competence*. On the surface the tests are based on the communicative language ability model and thus give an impression that the construct of speaking ability has some solid theoretical foundations; but in reality they represent a semidirect OPI test. From the validity point of view, we do not know what these tests measure—communicative speaking language ability or language speaking proficiency.

The social consequences of this state of confusion as to the ultimate purpose of the TSE and SPEAK tests are also visible. For example, some academic institutions, such as Arizona State University, allow the ITA to choose between the TSE/SPEAK and their own in-house assessment of speaking ability. That is, in place of the TSE or SPEAK test, the ITA is allowed to conduct a fifteen-minute classroom activity that is videotaped and then rated by university instructors. The rating obtained on this new form of speaking assessment is viewed as comparable to the rating obtained on the SPEAK or TSE test. As I was unofficially informed, the rating obtained on this new in-house test is considered to be more informative as to the ITA's future performance in the classroom than the rating obtained on the TSE or SPEAK test; therefore, the ITAs are encouraged to take this test. The development of such new tests seems to reflect a general social dissatisfaction with the current tests of second language speaking ability that claim to be based on the theoretical models of communicative competence.

## An Alternative Framework: Interactional Competence Theory

Some researchers working in the fields of second language theory and testing have also voiced their dissatisfaction with current communicative models. Hall (1993, 1995), He and Young (1998), and Young (1999) propose an alternative theoretical framework to communicative competence. They propose a new theoretical framework—interactional competence theory—as a replacement for communicative competence.

Interactional competence is "a theory of the knowledge that participants bring to and realize in interaction and includes an account of how this knowledge is acquired"

(Young 1999: 118). The domain of this theory is face-to-face interaction, which makes the theory relevant to our discussion of what speaking ability is.

The fundamental principle of interactional competence theory is the notion of coconstruction defined as "The joint creation of a form, interpretations, stance, action, activity, identity, skill, ideology, emotion, or other culturally meaningful reality" (Jacoby and Ochs 1995: 171). The notion of coconstruction has an impact on the view of second language knowledge. Contrary to communicative competence theory, as elaborated by Bachman (1990) and Canale and Swain (1980), knowledge of language within interactional competence theory is viewed not as a cognitive property of a single individual, but as jointly created by all participants in interaction (He and Young 1998; Young 1999). Coconstruction need not automatically imply a friendly coconstruction. As Jacoby and Ochs (1995) point out, a debate or argument is just as coconstructed as a friendly dialogue or a conversation.

Another fundamental principle of interactional competence theory, which drastically differs from communicative competence, pertains to the notion of general language competence. According to interactional competence theory, general competence does not exist, only local to specific contexts competence exists. These specific contexts of interactions are called "oral interactive practices" (Hall 1993, 1995).

Hall's definition of oral interactive practices is very similar to Hymes's (1974) definition of communicative speech event. Hall (1993: 144) defines oral interactive practices as speech events that are "socioculturally conventionalized configurations of face-to-face interaction by which and within which group members communicate." Interactional competence, thus, is jointly created and locally situated in interactive practices.

According to Hall, interactional competence is acquired in three steps, or through three processes. The first process pertains to "the discovery (other- and self-guided) of interactive patterns in the practices in which we engage with others"; the second process is connected with "observation and reflection on others' participatory moves and the responses to these moves"; and the last process involves "our own active constructions of responses to these patterns" (Hall 1995: 218). These three processes can be simply summarized as observation, reflection, and creation.

During these three processes, the individual acquires many resources of various types, such as vocabulary and syntax, knowledge of how to manage turns and topics, and knowledge of rhetorical scripts and skills (Young 1999; Hall 1993, 1995). These resources and skills can then be generalized to the same type of interactive practices. For example, once the individual acquires the interactional competence to participate in a conversation, he/she will be able to transfer this knowledge to different conversations.

To summarize, interactional competence theory is a theory of knowledge. It specifies the type of knowledge one has to possess in order to participate in interactive practices. It is also a theory of second language acquisition because it identifies processes that lead to the acquisition of essential resources indispensable for the development and use of locally situated and jointly constructed interactional competence. The main domain of interactional competence theory is face-to-face interaction.

The interactional competence framework proposes a view of interaction that is diametrically opposed to the communicative competence framework. That is, it proposes a social view of interaction. This social view of interaction presents a challenge to current speaking tests in which the examinee is solely responsible for the performance (McNamara 1996; Johnson 2000).

Although interactional competence theory offers important insights into the nature of second language ability (speaking in particular), it neglects, however, to admit the roots of its ideas. The knowledge of these roots is essential for our understanding and appreciation of the complexity of the ideas included in the theory. Interactional competence theory has not developed in a vacuum. It is based on the work of researchers like Vygotsky, Bakhtin, and Bourdieu. Simply speaking, interactional competence has been developed on "borrowed" ideas, and the origin of these ideas should be acknowledged and recognized. The understanding of these historical roots is extremely important because they lay foundations for our critical appraisal of the entire interactional competence theory. That is, understanding of the roots allows us to evaluate the appropriateness of applying some of the borrowed concepts to the interactional competence framework.

The roots of the fundamental principles of interactional competence can be primarily traced back to the work of the Soviet psychologist Vygotsky (1978, 1981), the work of his contemporary colleague Bakhtin (1981, 1986), and the work of the French sociologist Bourdieu (1991), who developed an innovative approach to language called "theory of practice," in which he introduced ideas similar to Hall's interactive practices under the name of "habitus." The habitus is a set of dispositions (similar to Hall's resources and skills) that are acquired through participation in social interactions and are transferable to different social interactions of a similar type.

Vygotsky's sociocultural theory offers a more comprehensive view of language ability than interactional competence frameworks, which I consider to be part of his sociocultural theory. Vygotsky's sociocultural theory offers a unified theoretical framework for the entire second language field, that is, second language theory and research, second language teaching, and second language testing. It offers a new understanding of what second language ability is, what type of knowledge it requires, how it is acquired, and how it should be taught and measured. In my view, Vygotsky's theory provides the best theoretical and practical answers to the second question of my book: What is speaking ability? Therefore, in the last chapter I shall describe the main tenets of Vygotsky's sociocultural theory and discuss its implications for second language testing and, in particular, speaking.

# Chapter 9

# THE PRACTICAL ORAL LANGUAGE ABILITY: THE APPLICATION OF VYGOTSKY'S SOCIOCULTURAL THEORY TO LANGUAGE TESTING

The Soviet psychologist Lev S. Vygotsky (1896–1934) wrote extensively on the issues pertaining to cognitive and educational psychology, philosophy, semiotics, and psycholinguistics. He advocated interdisciplinary connections among various branches of knowledge as the only means for achieving scientific progress. The interdisciplinary nature of Vygotsky's work has appealed to a wide range of scientific branches of knowledge.

For some time now, such scholars as Lantolf and Appel (1998), van Lier (1996), Lantolf and Pavlenko (1995),

Aljaafreh and Lantolf (1994), and Schinke-Llano (1993) have been applying Vygotsky's ideas, in particular his sociocultural theory, to second language acquisition theory and instruction. Despite the popularity of Vygotsky's theory in second language acquisition and teaching, little interest has been shown by the testing community in Vygotsky's sociocultural theory. To my knowledge, only two authors, McNamara (1996) and Johnson (2000), have acknowledged the value of Vygotsky's sociocultural framework for second language testing.

In this chapter, I shall describe some fundamental principles of Vygotsky's sociocultural theory and discuss their relevance for second language testing, particularly in the area of speaking ability. Vygotsky's sociocultural theory represents, in my opinion, an important theoretical framework for second language theory and practice; it provides an explanation of what language ability is and how it is acquired. Vygotsky's sociocultural framework can provide "theoretical rationales" in support of "the adequacy and appropriateness of inferences and actions based on the test score" (Messick 1989: 13). These theoretical rationales could, in turn, help to promote appropriate empirical investigations of the validity of such inferences. Vygotsky's theoretical framework can supply important foundations for a new construct of second language ability—speaking ability, in particular.

## Key Concepts of Vygotsky's Sociocultural Theory

Vygotsky's sociocultural theory of mind can be summarized in terms of three main tenets or themes (Wertsch 1990, 1985):

1. the developmental analysis of mental processes;
2. the social origin of human mental functions;
3. the role of language (that is, a system of signs) in the development of human cognitive functions.

Note that the three concepts are very closely interrelated and that the understanding of one requires a full understanding of the others and the way they interact with one another.

The first key concept refers to the type of analysis that Vygotsky advocates for appropriate investigations, understandings, and interpretations of the higher forms of human mental functions. Vygotsky (1978: 64–67) states, "We need to concentrate on not the *product* of development but on the very *process* by which higher forms are established. To encompass in research the process of a given thing's development and all its phases and changes—from birth to death—fundamentally means to discover its nature, its essence." Thus, to discover how human mental functions work, we ought to focus on *processes* and changes, their origin and genetic history (that is, developmental transformation), and not on the final product of development.

Vygotsky views the ontogenesis of development of children in terms of two forces: natural, or biological, which is responsible for the lower level mental functions; and cultural, which is responsible for the higher mental functions. According to Vygotsky (1978), what distinguishes lower mental functions from higher mental functions is the degree of regulation. That is, lower mental functions are regulated by the environment and higher mental functions are self-regulated: "The central characteristic of elementary functions is that they are totally and directly determined by stimulation from the environment. For higher functions, the central feature is self-generated stimulation, that is, the creation and use of artificial stimuli which become the immediate causes" (Vygotsky 1978: 39).

The ontogenesis of development of the child may be described in terms of three stages delineated by the degree of control over the mental processes. In the first stage, the object-regulated stage, the child is controlled by the environment; in the second stage, the other-regulated stage, the child's mental functions depend on the assistance of and collaboration with other people; and in the final stage, the self-regulated stage, the child takes control over his/her higher mental processes. The object-regulated stage is the result of the operation of natural forces. The arrival at the self-regulated stage is the result of the operation of cultural forces. That is, cultural forces account for the higher mental functions. Cultural forces are discussed in more detail in the second tenet of Vygotsky's sociocultural theory of mind.

The second tenet of Vygotsky's sociocultural theory claims that higher mental functions, such as voluntary attention, planning, monitoring, rational thought, and learning, originate in social activity. This claim is captured in the *genetic law of cultural development:*

> Any function in the child's cultural development appears twice or on two planes. First it appears on the social plane, and then on the psychological plane. First it appears between people as an interpsychological category, and then within the child as an intrapsychological category. This is equally true with regard to voluntary attention, logical memory, the formation of concepts, and the development of volition. We may consider this position as a law in the full sense of the word, but it goes without saying that internalization transforms the process itself and changes its structure and functions. Social relations or relations among people genetically underlie all higher functions and their relationships. (Vygotsky 1981: 163)

According to the genetic law of cultural development, higher level mental processes originate on the social plane (that is, interpersonal), external to the individual plane. Individuals internalize many patterns of social activities, which they observe and participate in on the interpersonal plane. The process of internalization, however, should not be viewed as a mere copying of the external processes because, as the above quote indicates, "internalization transforms the process itself and changes its structure and functions" (Vygotsky 1981: 163). That is, the internal processes reflect the external processes, but they are not identical because during the process of internalization the external processes are transformed and changed. Though not identical, these two processes—interpersonal and intrapersonal—are closely interrelated.

The transition from the interpersonal to the intrapersonal plane is a very dynamic, gradual, and ever-changing process that takes place within the zone of proximal development (ZPD). Vygotsky develops the notion of the ZPD to address two specific and practical problems, the problem of assessment in education and the problem of teaching practices. According to Vygotsky, the existing forms of assessment and teaching practices focus solely on the individual's actual level of cognitive development, and they neglect to take into consideration another level of the individual's cognitive development: his/her *potential* level of development. Vygotsky (1978: 86) defines the ZPD as follows: "It is the distance between the actual developmental level as determined by independent problem solving and the level of potential development as determined through problem solving under adult guidance or in collaboration with more capable peers."

Vygotsky is more interested in the individual's potential level of development than in the individual's actual level of development. In his view, the potential level is more indicative of the individual's mental growth than the actual level. Vygotsky (1978: 86) calls this potential level of development "buds . . . rather than the fruits of development," which are "not yet matured but are in the process of maturation." Two individuals, for example, may be at the same actual level of development as determined by their final test scores, but their ZPDs may differ, reflected by their differing ability to solve problems during collaboration, or *interaction,* with a more capable peer or an adult. Vygotsky views interaction within the ZPD as the key element for the individual's mental development.

The third fundamental tenet of Vygotsky's sociocultural theory pertains to the role of signs, in particular to the role of a symbolic system of signs—language—in the development of the higher mental functions. For Vygotsky, the transition from the interpersonal plane to the intrapersonal plane is dependent on the mediated function of language.

Language represents not a system of abstract syntactic rules, as in Chomsky's tradition, but *speech,* whose main function is to facilitate human communication. In addition to this communicative function, speech plays a crucial role in the transition from the interpersonal to the intrapersonal plane; therefore, speech plays an important role in the development of the higher mental functions, such as learning.

The transition from the interpersonal plane to the intrapersonal plane is signaled by the emergence of so-called egocentric speech. The emergence of egocentric speech is important because it reveals some insights as to the working of the higher mental functions. Egocentric speech also signals that the individual is ready to move toward a self-regulated stage. When the transition from the interpersonal plane (that is, between people) to the intrapersonal plane (within the individual) is completed, egocentric speech disappears and takes the form of inner speech, whose function is to facilitate internal or intellectual dialogue on the intrapersonal plane.

To summarize, Vygotsky's sociocultural theory accounts for the role of society, culture, and institutions in the development of human higher mental functions. Vygotsky's theory undermines the *universal* or innate approach, which claims that an innate human mechanism is solely responsible for human mental development. In contrast to the universal approach, Vygotsky's sociocultural theory claims that social, institutional, and cultural environments are instrumental in human mental growth. An individual's mental functions reflect the social, cultural, and institutional settings to which the individual has been exposed during the course of his/her life.

As Wertsch (1985, 1990) points out, the short life of Vygotsky did not allow him to pursue the investigation of the effect of various social and institutional settings on mental development. At the end of his life, however, Vygotsky was very much interested in finding the connection between speech characteristics of various social and institutional settings and their effects on the individual's mental development. He was especially interested in investigating the link between speech characteristics of academic settings and certain types of mental development that the exposure to these environments triggers. These relative "shortcomings" of Vygotsky's sociocultural theory may be remedied by borrowing some concepts from the work of his contemporary, Bakhtin, who is important for our understanding of the roots of interactional competence theory (Wertsch 1985, 1990).

Mikhail Bakhtin (1885–1975) worked in the field of literary criticism, and his literary theory includes such concepts as speech genre, voice, and dialogue. Like Vygotsky, Bakhtin (1981, 1986) refuses to view language as an abstract system of signs devoid of social, historical, cultural, and institutional contexts. For Bakhtin, language is a living thing, and as a living thing, it reflects and defines at the same time the various contexts in which it is used. Language always lies on

> the border between oneself and the other. The word in language is half someone's. It becomes "one's own" only when the speaker populates it with his own intention, his own semantic and expressive intention. Prior to this moment of appropriation, the word does not

exist in a neutral and impersonal language (it is not, after all, out of a dictionary that the speaker gets his words!), but rather it exits in other people's mouths, in other people's contexts, serving other people's intentions: it is from there that one must take the word, and make it one's own. (Bakhtin 1981: 293–94).

When we speak, we speak not with one language; we speak with many "languages," we speak with many *voices*. These voices reflect the social, cultural, and institutional environments we have been exposed to in the course of our lives. Our own voices reflect these various contexts because this is how the process of "appropriation" (internalization) begins. Only through exposure to these various contexts can we acquire different voices, which are essential for human communication.

Bakhtin (1981: 262–63) categorizes these voices into *social speech types* such as: "social dialects, characteristic group behavior, professional jargons, generic languages, languages of generations and age groups, tendentious languages, languages of the authorities, of various circles and of passing fashions, languages that serve the specific sociopolitical purposes of the day, even of the hour (each day has its own slogan, its own vocabulary, its own emphases)."

Social speech types can be even further categorized into *speech genre*. Bakhtin (1986: 78) claims that we speak only in "definite speech genres, that is, all our utterances have definite and relatively stable typical *forms of construction of speech genres,*" and we may not even be aware of it: "Like Molière's Monsieur Jourdain who, when speaking in prose, had no idea that was what he was doing, we speak in diverse genres without suspecting that they exist." In Bakhtin's view, not only do we speak in speech genres, but we hear in terms of speech genres as well. Thus, without speech genres, human communication would not be possible. Bakhtin (1986: 79) writes,

> We learn to cast our speech in generic forms and, when hearing other's speech, we guess its genre from the very first words; we predict a certain length (that is, its approximate length of the speech whole) and a certain compositional structure; we foresee the end; that is, from the very beginning we have a sense of the speech whole, which is only later differentiated during the speech process. If speech genres did not exist and we had not mastered them, if we had to originate them during the speech process and construct each utterance at will for the first time, speech communication would be almost impossible.

Like various social speech types, speech genres are acquired through the individual's exposure to a variety of social, cultural, and institutional contexts. The lack of exposure to a particular sociocultural or institutional context deprives the individual of the acquisition of speech genres typical of that setting.

Bakhtin's voices and speech genres are always in a dialogic relationship. In fact, Bakhtin places a dialogic relationship at the core of his literary theory. According to Bakhtin, we only "speak" in a form of a dialogue; even if we speak to ourselves, as in a monologue, we speak in a form of a dialogue. For Bakhtin, dialogue is not synonymous with the conventional meaning of a dialogue, which presupposes the presence of two interlocutors who take turns at producing utterances. For Bakhtin, every utterance, every voice, stands in a multiple dialogic relationship with other utterances, with other voices in a text, but since every utterance, every word, is "half someone's," this dialogic relationship extends to the original owner of the utterance, to the social, cultural, and institutional context in which it was originally situated.

To summarize, Bakhtin's concepts of speech genres, voices, and dialogues represent an important contribution to Vygotsky's sociocultural theory because they provide an explanation of how speech characteristics associated with various sociocultural settings account for the patterns of human mental growth. The exposure and practice within these various social, institutional, and cultural settings are crucial for acquiring many different voices. These voices affect the pattern of higher mental functions. That is, our voices reflect the sociocultural and institutional settings in which they have been acquired, and these voices, in turn, affect the way our higher mental functions are developed.

## Implications of Vygotsky's Sociocultural Theory for Second Language Acquisition (SLA) Research and Instruction

As mentioned earlier, some researchers working in the field of SLA consider Vygotsky's theory very compatible with SLA theories and instruction (Schinke-Llano 1993; Lantolf and Pavlenko 1995; van Lier 1996; and Lantolf and Appel 1998). This compatibility is visible in many areas. Like Vygotsky's first tenet, SLA is interested in the learner's developmental changes. SLA is also interested in the effects of various social, cultural, and institutional settings on the learner's second language acquisition. In particular, SLA is interested in the effect of one type of sociocultural and institutional setting, the classroom, on the learner's interlanguage development.

Some SLA researchers see the ZPD as a very useful paradigm within which both SLA research and theory can be conducted. For example, the transition from the interpersonal plane to the intrapersonal plane within the ZPD offers explanations as to how second language knowledge is acquired. Second language knowledge originates on the interpersonal, social plane before it is internalized on the intrapersonal plane. Also, the ZPD promotes research that investigates the effects of various types of classroom interactions on the learner's interlanguage development. For example, van Lier (1996) advocates the development of special types of tasks that promote the most efficient and most effective transition from the other-regulated to the self-regulated stage through classroom activities that increase the learner's confidence, encourage independence, promote language awareness, and motivate the learner.

Furthermore, van Lier (1996) views one type of interaction—conversation—as the most desirable and effective form of interaction for the learner's second language development in the classroom. In a typical language classroom interaction, the teacher is solely responsible for what is talked about, how it is talked about, and when and where it is talked about. This type of interaction does not promote the learner's active participation in the learning process. It prolongs the learner's reliance on others, and that in turn slows down his/her transition from the other-regulated stage to the self-regulated stage. The symmetrical distribution of rights and duties in conversations could change the existing dynamics in the classroom by making the learner become a more active and self-reliant participant in the learning process.

Adhering to Vygotsky's view of language as socioculturally and locally situated, van Lier (1996) encourages teachers and curriculum developers to design classroom activities that truly reflect the learner's real-world language needs. This reflection, however, should be based not on the teacher's intuition, but on solid empirical evidence. The classroom should not create its own interpretation of the reality; rather it should reflect it in its full social, cultural, and institutional complexity.

As indicated above, SLA theory and teaching have both found Vygotsky's sociocultural theory useful and theoretically compatible. I believe that the time has come for second language testing to give Vygotsky's theory serious consideration.

## Implications of Vygotsky's Sociocultural Theory for Language Testing

What are the theoretical and practical implications of Vygotsky's sociocultural theory for second language testing? First, from a theoretical point of view, his sociocultural theory claims there is no universal competence. There are only local competencies, which are situated is a variety of social, cultural, and institutional settings. Indeed, here Vygotsky's theory is consistent with the position advocated by the proponents of interactional competence theory, namely, that there is no general competence, only local competence. Local competence is acquired through a process of social interaction and through exposure to a wide variety of sociocultural and institutional settings. Exposure to many varied contexts allows one to acquire voices, that is, all the necessary verbal and nonverbal resources, that, once internalized, can be used in many contexts of the same type. If Vygotsky's claim were to be applied and found valid to language testing, then we should stop developing theoretical models of general language ability and start developing models that reflect local and sociocultural language competence.

Second, Vygotsky's sociocultural theory encourages us to develop new models that focus more on the learner's potential level than on his/her actual level of language ability. Some may argue that current language speaking tests like the OPI have already addressed this issue by including in their design the plus levels. Recall, however, that the OPI's plus levels are determined on the basis of the candidate's performance in the probes phase, whose purpose is to help the tester confirm the candidate's actual level of language ability, not his/her potential level of language ability. If Vygotsky's ideas regarding the learner's potential level of development were to be applied to language testing, then we would have to design a new test that elicits the learner's potential level of his/her language ability. Also, the new scale's level descriptions would have to include specific references to the candidate's potential level of language ability in relation to clearly defined and described sociocultural and institutional settings.

Third, if Vygotsky's framework were to be applied to language testing, then interaction would have to be viewed as a social, not a cognitive, issue. This switch from a cognitive to a social perspective would require a greater involvement on the tester's part, which would have to be consistent with the prototypical features of a given speech event. For example, if the tester were to play the role of the audience at a formal academic lecture, his/her involvement should be appropriate to this particular context. Since being an active participant in an interaction requires much attention to the local development of the interaction, the tester would have to be released from the responsibility of rating the candidate's performance. That is, the tester's primary responsibility would be to the social demands of the interaction at hand. The final rating of the candidate's performance would have to be performed by an independent tester(s)-observer(s) who would be required to assign the final rating based on the strength of the candidate's performance *in relation* to the tester's performance in the interaction. That is, the tester's performance should also be rated to determine its effect on the candidate's performance.

Fourth, if applied to second language testing, Vygotsky's sociocultural theory would have a great impact on existing scales. Recall that Bachman and Palmer's (1983) scales of communicative language ability are defined "with no reference to specific contextual features" (Bachman 1990: 329). Within this new framework, such scales would not be acceptable because contextual features represent the necessary ingredient in our ability to assess the learner's context-specific second language ability. Neither would the scales be similar to the ACTFL/ETS/ILR, despite the fact that these include the notion of context in their scales.

The ACTFL/ETS/ILR would be unacceptable because they hold the view that contexts could be graded, that is, ranked in terms of their level of difficulty. Recall that ACTFL/ETS/ILR scales are progressive: each level subsumes the previous level, and the higher the level, the higher the level of difficulty. Thus, the selected contexts for the OPI level 4 are considered to be more "demanding" than the contexts included in the OPI level 2. In this scale system, contexts are "normalized" as to their difficulty levels so that they can be arbitrarily distributed among levels. The application of Vygotsky's framework would end the era of scales similar to existing oral language proficiency scales, which include criteria that do not exist in reality (like an idealized well-educated native speaker), and communicative language ability scales, which assume the existence of general "universal" language ability.

Because Vygotsky's theory stresses the local nature of language knowledge, its application would require that language testing instruments be locally developed and interpreted. The institutions that make evaluative decisions would be encouraged to become self-reliant and self-regulated. The interpretation of test scores would also have to be locally determined, and the ability to generalize the scores would be possible only from one local context to another of the same type.

As a practical example, in the last section of my book I shall describe in some detail how I envision the development of language speaking tests based on Vygotsky's framework. I propose to call these speaking tests the Practical Oral Language Ability (POLA).

1. The purpose of the Practical Oral Language Ability test should be clearly stated, and the intended audience should be clearly defined. For example, "The purpose of this test is to assess the speaking ability of the ITA in a variety of academic contexts."

2. Major interactive oral events or practices typical of a given sociocultural or institutional setting should be clearly identified and described. The identification and description should be based on a thorough internal needs analysis. For example, in our hypothetical academic context with the ITA as a targeted audience, the following interactive oral events could be identified: office hours, group discussions, and lectures.

3. Each selected interactive oral event ought to be carefully analyzed in terms of its main functions, tasks, abilities, and skills. For example, in our hypothetical academic institutional context, during office hours, the ITA may be required to offer some academic advice, explain a concept or a technical term, and provide assistance with homework. During lectures, the ITA may be required to rephrase, describe, and illustrate abstract and technical terms; the ITA may be required to synthesize information by using appropriate linguistics and nonlinguistics resources such as charts, tables, and so on. Also, the ITA may be expected to be able to

tell a joke or a funny story. Lectures as a speech event are considered to be asymmetrical in terms of the participant's rights and duties. The ability to tell a joke, for instance, may be viewed as a useful skill for defusing this unequal distribution of power in a lecture. It is important to note that not all selected functions and tasks need to be linguistic in nature. For example, the task of counseling students may require some abilities that go beyond language ability, such as the ability to listen.

4. The selected functions and tasks for each interactive oral event should be graded according to their importance and relevance for a given sociocultural and institutional setting. In a lecture, for instance, the ability to tell a joke could be valued as less important than the ability to synthesize or analyze or to produce a coherent, cogent text.

5. Once the selection of major functions and tasks for each selected interactive oral event is completed, the decision regarding its format should be made. The format of each interactive oral event should resemble as closely as possible its real-life format. Depending on the available resources and local institutional and social needs, however, the format of some of the selected interactive oral practices may be adjusted. For example, it may not be feasible to ask the ITA to give a lecture in front of a real-life audience, so the tester may be asked to play the role of an audience. Also, it is possible that more than one format could be selected. For example, an office hour interactive oral practice may take the format of an interview and/or a conversation. Within this new framework, the format of each interac-

tive oral practice would be different. That is, the application of this new framework to testing speaking ability would end the era of the OPI tests, in which different tasks and functions embedded in different sociocultural and institutional settings are evaluated within one arbitrarily constructed OPI format.

6. Each interactive oral event should be rated separately and independently of the other events. The evaluation of each selected interactive oral event could be as simple as pass or fail or it could be measured on a scale that describes in detail the strengths and weaknesses of the candidate's language ability as to each identified function or task within each interactive oral event. For example, the ITA's performance in a lecture could be rated on the basis of his/her ability to explain, synthesize, produce a coherent text, and so forth. Criterial levels of performance within each interactive oral event should be based on local sociocultural and institutional needs.

7. If possible, there should be a group of evaluators (two or more) responsible for rating the candidate's performance within each interactive oral event. These evaluators should not be responsible for participating in each oral event. This responsibility would be assigned to the tester or testers who would be required to actively participate in each interactive oral event and who would be released from the responsibility of rating the candidate's performance. These interactive oral events should be videotaped for the purpose of being rated later on by a group of evaluators.

8. The selection and training of testers should be based on their ability to participate in a variety of interactive oral events. That is, the tester's abilities, skills, and personality should be taken into consideration during the tester's selection process. Not only should the candidate's performance be rated, but the tester's performance within each selected event should be evaluated as well. Recall that within this new framework, interaction is viewed as a social, not cognitive, issue, and the candidate's speaking language ability in each interactive event is dependent on the tester's performance.

9. To ensure the tester's active and appropriate participation in each interactive oral event, the tester should be exposed to a wide variety of speech events during tester training workshops. The prototypical features of such major speech events as an interview or a conversation should be discussed in a tester training workshop. For example, the tester should be made aware of the fact that in an everyday conversation, participants have equal rights and duties in topic negation and turn taking. Also, in tester training workshops, the tester ought to be informed about the ultimate purpose of each selected interactive oral event and be reminded about its real-life connections. This real-life connection is essential for the tester's ability to appropriately elicit the necessary language samples from the candidate. In current OPI systems, for example, the purposes of certain tasks and functions are so vaguely defined that testers are forced to define them by themselves. Because

most the OPI testers are language teachers, not surprisingly their definitions are primarily based on their language classroom experiences, and their ratings are based on the candidate's grammatical knowledge. Also, a clear understanding of the ultimate goal of each selected event is essential for the tester's ability to direct the interaction in such a way that the candidate is able to demonstrate his/her full language potential.

10. The feedback provided to the candidate within this new system could be very practical and informative. For example, if the candidate happened to demonstrate some problems within the lecture, the candidate could be advised to observe this concrete real-life speech event. In addition, the feedback to the candidate can be fine-tuned by directing his/her attention to a specific feature or features of a given speech situation. For example, the ITA may be asked to focus on the way cohesion and coherence are accomplished in lectures. This type of feedback can be more informative and useful to the candidate than the feedback the candidate receives on such current speaking tests as the OPI. For example, if the OPI candidate is asked to improve his/her ability to hypothesize, which is one of the required tasks in level 3, this type of feedback could be of less help than if the candidate were told that he/she needs to improve the ability to hypothesize in the context of a formal interview in which the candidate is expected to express opinions and solutions on the topic of his/her expertise, as is typically done during political interviews.

11. As mentioned earlier, within this system, language competence is locally situated. In our hypothetical ITA situation, we could say, for instance, that the ITA has a speaking language ability sufficient to participate in conversations and group discussions, conduct office hours, and give lectures, or that the ITS has a speaking ability sufficient to participate in all selected interactive events except for lectures. In addition, depending on the scale used to measure the candidate's performance in each interactive oral event, we may provide a more detailed description of the candidate's speaking ability in each selected interactive oral practice. We would not be able, however, to make general comments as to the candidate's overall second language speaking ability. This could be illustrated as in figure 9.1.

12. Although we would not be able to make general statements regarding the candidate's speaking ability independent of a given context, we would, nevertheless, be able to make practical decisions

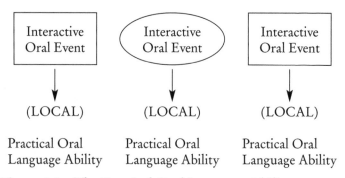

Figure 9.1   The Practical Oral Language Ability

regarding the candidate's ability to fulfill second language speaking requirements within the confines of institutional or sociocultural settings. For example, if the ITA were not able to perform certain functions during lectures, such as offer an explanation, but he/she was able to provide some explanations during office hours or during a group discussion, the ITA may still be offered the position based on the fact that he/she has some potential ability. Or the ITA may be given some partial responsibility; that is, the ITA may be asked to perform all of the ITA's duties except for giving lectures, or the ITA may not be offered the position if his/her main responsibility in this academic institution relies heavily on an ability to conduct lectures. Although language competence is viewed as being locally situated in well-defined sociocultural and institutional settings, some local competencies are more universal than others. For example, language competence sufficient to give a lecture in an academic setting will not differ much from that required to give a lecture in a business setting. The same pertains to a conversation or an interview. But these similarities cannot be assumed automatically. After all, participating in a conversation with students during office hours is not the same as participating in a conversation with the president of the United States.

Vygotsky's sociocultural model challenges current testing paradigms; it forces us to look at language ability from a different perspective, from a sociocultural and institutional perspective—from a local perspective. It empowers the consumer to take control over the process of developing and interpreting test results. The time has come for the testing community to seriously consider a new paradigm for what second language ability is; the time has come to give the Vygotskian theory serious consideration.

The theoretical rationales and empirical findings presented in the discourse analysis study and the native speaker's perception study provided quantitative and qualitative evidence for what oral language ability is within the OPI testing model. Dissatisfaction with the findings led to building a new theory for defining and assessing oral language ability.

I believe that the purpose of a theory is not to provide all the answers, but to provide a focus for investigation, a point of reference. I hope that this new theory will become a useful point of reference for future discussions and investigations of what oral language ability is and how it should be assessed.

# OPI CODING SHEET
## (*SAMPLE*)

| Floor Turn | Speaker | Turn Unit | Turn Allocation | Repair Type | Repair Location | New Topic Nomination | Topic Change Natural | Topic Change Contrived | Question Type | Discourse Unit |
|---|---|---|---|---|---|---|---|---|---|---|
| 1 | | | | | | | | | | |
| 2 | | | | | | | | | | |
| 3 | | | | | | | | | | |
| 4 | | | | | | | | | | |
| 5 | | | | | | | | | | |
| 6 | | | | | | | | | | |
| 7 | | | | | | | | | | |
| 8 | | | | | | | | | | |
| 9 | | | | | | | | | | |
| 10 | | | | | | | | | | |

# CODING DOCUMENT

## 1. FLOOR TURN

*Turn unit construction*

    1. laughing/silence/exclamation/surprise, etc.

    2. backchannel

    3. lexicon

    4. phrases

    5. question(s)

    6. utterance

    7. utterances

    8. utterance(s) followed by question(s)

    9. question(s) followed by utterance(s)

*Turn allocation at the Transition Relevance Point:*

    1. current speaker continues/select self

    2. current speaker selects next

    3. noncurrent speaker selects self

## 2. REPAIR

*Repair type:*
    1. Self-initiated self-repaired
    2. Self-initiated other-repaired
    3. Other-initiated self-repaired
    4. Other-initiated other-repaired

*Repair location*
    1. Same Floor Turn
    2. Transition Relevance Point
    3. Next Floor turn

## 3. TOPIC

*New Topic Nomination*
    1. Tester
    2. Candidate

*Topic Change*
    1. Natural
    2. Contrived

*Topic Change Method*
    1. interruption
    2. question/role-play/task
    3. example/explanation of testing procedures
    4. digression/jokes
    5. no response
    6. answer/response/statement

7. external circumstances (coughs/sneezes)
8. summary/return to the same subject matter
9. preclosing
10. closing

## 4. QUESTION TYPES

1. information seeking
2. information checking
3. clarification
4. comprehension
5. confirmation

## 5. DISCOURSE UNIT

1. The tester asks questions, the candidate answers
2. The tester asks questions, the candidate answers, the tester provides feedback/makes comments
3. The candidate asks questions, the tester answers
4. The tester and the candidate alternate in asking and answering questions/making comments
5. The tester presents tasks, role-plays, and the candidate responds
6. The tester asks question(s), the candidate answers, the tester provides feedback and introduces a new question/role-play/task
7. The tester explains testing procedures

# Bibliography

Adams, M. L. "Measuring Foreign Language Speaking Proficiency: A Study of Agreement Among Raters." In *Direct Testing Speaking Proficiency: Theory and Applications,* edited by John L. D. Clark, 129–49. Princeton: Educational Testing Service, 1978.

Aljaafreh, Ali, and James P. Lantolf. "Negative Feedback as Regulation and Second Language Learning in the Zone of Proximal Development." *Modern Language Journal* 78 (1994): 455–83.

Allwright, Richard L., and Kathleen Bailey. *Focus on the Language Classroom.* Cambridge: Cambridge University Press, 1991.

American Council on the Teaching of Foreign Languages. *ACTFL Proficiency Guidelines.* New York: American Council on the Teaching of Foreign Languages, 1986.

Austin, John. *How to Do Things with Words.* Oxford: Oxford University Press, 1962.

Bachman, Lyle F. "Problems in Examining the Validity of the ACTFL Oral Proficiency Interview." *Studies in Second Language Acquisition* 10 (1988): 149–74.

———. *Fundamental Considerations in Language Testing.* Oxford: Oxford University Press, 1990.

Bachman, Lyle F., and Sandra J. Savignon. "The Evaluation of Communicative Language Proficiency: A Critique of the ACTFL Oral Interview." *Modern Language Journal* 70, no. 4 (1986): 380–390.

Bachman, Lyle F., and Adrian S. Palmer. *Language Testing in Practice.* Oxford: Oxford University Press, 1996.

———, and Andrew D. Cohen, eds. *Interfaces Between Second Language Acquisition and Language Testing Research.* Cambridge: Cambridge University Press, 1998.

Bakhtin, Mikhail M. *The Dialogic Imagination.* Edited by Michael Holquist. Austin: University of Texas Press. 1981.

———. *Speech Genres and Other Late Essays.* Translated by Vern McGee. Austin: University of Texas Press, 1986.

Bourdieu, Pierre. *Language and Symbolic Power.* Edited by John B. Thompson. Cambridge: Polity Press, 1991.

Briggs, Charles. *Learning How to Ask.* Cambridge: Cambridge University Press, 1986.

Brown, Gillian, and George Yule. *Discourse Analysis.* Cambridge: Cambridge University Press, 1983.

Brown, Penelope, and Stephan Levinson. *Politeness: Some Universals in Language Usage.* Cambridge: Cambridge University Press, 1987.

Byrnes, Heidi. "Proficiency as a Framework for Research in Second Language Acquisition." *Modern Language Journal* 7, no. 1 (1987): 44–49.

Canale, Michael. "From Communicative Competence to Communicative Language Pedagogy." In *Language and Communication*, edited by Jack Richards and Richard Schmidt, 2–27. Longman: London, 1983.

Canale, Michael, and Merril Swain. "Theoretical Bases of Communicative Approaches to Second Language Teaching and Testing." *Applied Linguistics* 1 (1980): 1–47.

Chapelle, Carol A. "Is a C-Test Valid for L2 Vocabulary Research?" *Second Language Research* 10 (1994): 157–87.

———. "Validity in Language Assessment." *Annual Review of Applied Linguistics* 19 (1999): 245–72.

Chaudron, Craig. *Second Language Classrooms: Research on Teaching and Learning*. Cambridge: Cambridge University Press, 1988.

Chomsky, Noam. *Aspects of the Theory of Syntax*. MIT Press, 1965.

Clark, John L. D. *Foreign Language Testing: Theory and Practice*. Philadelphia: Center for Curriculum Development, 1972.

———, ed. *Direct Testing of Speaking Proficiency: Theory and Application*. Princeton: Educational Testing Service, 1978a.

———. "Interview Testing Research at Educational Testing Service." In *Direct Testing of Speaking Proficiency: Theory and Application*. Princeton: Educational Testing Service, 1978b.

———. "Towards a Common Measure of Speaking Ability." In *Measuring Spoken Language Proficiency*. Washington: Georgetown University Press, 1980.

———. *A Study of the Comparability of Speaking Proficiency Interview Ratings Across Three Government Language Training Agencies*. Washington: Center for Applied Linguistics, 1986.

Clark, John L. D., and Ray T. Clifford. "The FSI/ILR/ACTFL Proficiency Scales and Testing Techniques: Development, Current Status, and Needed Research." *Studies in Second Language Acquisition* 10 (1988): 129–47.

———, and John Lett. "A Research Agenda." In *Second Language Proficiency Assessment: Current Issues,* edited by Pardee Lowe and Charles W. Stansfield, 53–82. Englewood Cliffs: Prentice-Hall Regents, 1988.

Cronbach, Lee J. *Essentials of Psychological Testing.* 4th ed. New York: Harper and Row, 1984.

Dandonoli, Patricia, and Grant Henning. "An Investigation of the Construct Validity of the ACTFL Proficiency Guidelines and Oral Proficiency Procedure." *Foreign Language Annals* 23 (1990): 11–22.

Davidson, Fred, and Brian Lynch. *Testcraft: Writing and Using Language Test Specifications.* New Haven: Yale University Press, forthcoming.

Educational Testing Service. *Oral Proficiency Testing Manual.* Princeton: Educational Testing Service, 1982.

———. *Speaking Proficiency English Assessment Kit: Rater Training Kit.* Princeton: Educational Testing Service, 1996.

———. *TOEIC Language Proficiency Interview Manual.* Princeton: Educational Testing Service, 1996.

Ellis, Rod. *Instructed Second Language Acquisition.* Oxford: Basil Blackwell, 1991.

Erickson, Frederick, and Jeffrey Schultz. *The Counselor as Gatekeeper: Social Interactions in Interviews.* New York: Academic Press, 1982.

Fanselow, John F. "The Treatment of Error in Oral Work." *Foreign Language Annals* 10 (1977): 583–93.

Ferguson, Charles A. "Towards a Characterization of English Foreigner Talk." *Anthropological Linguistics* 17 (1975): 1–14.

Flanders, Ned. *Analyzing Teaching Behavior.* Reading, Mass.: Addison-Wesley, 1970.

Gardner, Robert, and Wallace Lambert. *Attitudes and Motivation in Second Language Learning.* Rowley, Mass.: Newbury House, 1972.

Garfinkel, Harold. *Studies in Ethnomethodology.* Englewood Cliffs: Prentice-Hall, 1967.

Gaskill, William H. "Correction in Native Speaker–Non-Native Speaker Conversation." In *Discourse Analysis in Second Language Research,* edited by Jack Richards and Richard Schmidt, 125–13. Rowley, Mass.: Newbury House, 1989.

Goffman, Erving. *Interaction Ritual: Essays on Face-to-Face Behavior.* New York: Anchor Books, 1967.

———. *Frame Analysis.* New York: Harper and Row, 1974.

———. "Replies and Responses." *Language in Society* 5 (1976): 254–313.

———. *Forms of Talk.* Philadelphia: University of Pennsylvania Press, 1981.

Goodwin, Charles, and Alessandro Duranti. "Rethinking Context: An Introduction." In *Rethinking Context: Language as an Interactive Phenomenon,* edited by Alessandro Duranti and Charles Goodwin, 1–42. Cambridge: Cambridge University Press, 1992.

Goodwin, Charles, and Marjorie H. Goodman. "Assessments and Construction of Context." In *Rethinking Context: Language as an Interactive Phenomenon,* edited by Alessandro Duranti, and Charles Goodwin, 147–90. Cambridge: Cambridge University Press, 1992.

Grice, H. Paul. "Logic and Conversation." In *Syntax and Semantic,* edited by P. Cole and J. Morgan, 41–58. New York: Academia Press, 1975.

Gumperz, John J. *Discourse Strategies.* Cambridge: Cambridge University Press, 1982.

Hall, Joan K. "The Role of Oral Practices in Interaction with Implications for Learning Another Language." *Applied Linguistics* 14 (1993): 145–66.

———. "(Re)creating Our Worlds with Words: A Sociocultural Perspective of Face-to-Face Interaction." *Applied Linguistics* 16 (1995): 206–32.

Halliday, Michael A. K. *Explorations in the Functions of Language.* New York: Elsevier North-Holland, 1973.

Halliday, Michael A. K., and Ruquaiya Hasan. *Cohesion in English.* Cambridge: Cambridge University Press, 1976.

Hatch, Evelyn. *Discourse Analysis and Language Education.* Cambridge: Cambridge University Press, 1992.

He, Agnes, and Richard Young. "Language Proficiency Interviews: A Discourse Approach." In *Talking and Testing: Discourse Approaches to the Assessment of Oral Proficiency,* edited by Richard Young and Agnes He, 1–24. Amsterdam: John Benjamins, 1998.

Higgs, Theodore V., and Ray T. Clifford. "The Push Towards Communication." In *Curriculum, Competence and the Foreign Language Teacher,* edited by Theodore V. Higgs, 51–79. Skokie, Ill.: National Textbook, 1982.

Hughes, Arthur. *Testing for Language Teachers.* Cambridge: Cambridge University Press, 1989.

Hymes, Dell. "On Communicative Competence." In *Sociolinguistics,* edited by John B. Pride and Janet Holems, 269–93. Harmondsworth, Middlesex: Penguin, 1972.

————. *Foundations in Sociolinguistics: An Ethnographic Approach.* Philadelphia: Pennsylvania University Press, 1974.

Jakobson, Roman. "Linguistics and Poetics." In *The Structuralists: From Marx to Lévi-Strauss,* edited by Richard De George and Fernande De George, 85–122. Garden City, N.Y.: Anchor Books, 1972.

Jacoby, Sally, and Elinor Ochs. "Co-construction: An Introduction." *Research on Language and Social Interaction* 28 (1995): 171–83.

Johnson, Marysia. "What Kind of Speech Event is the Oral Proficiency Interview: Problems of Construct Validity." Ph.D. diss., Georgetown University, 1997. Abstract in Dissertation Abstract International 58–09A (1998) 3492.

————. "Interaction in the Oral Proficiency Interview: Problems of Validity." *Pragmatics* 10, no. 2 (2000): 215–31.

Johnson, Marysia, and Andrea Tyler. "Re-analyzing the OPI: How Much Does it Look like Natural Conversation?" In *Taking and Testing: Discourse Approaches to the Assessment of Oral Proficiency,* edited by Richard Young and Agnes He, 27–51. Amsterdam: Benjamins, 1998.

Jones, Edward E., and Harold B. Gerard. *Foundation of Social Psychology.* New York: Wiley, 1967.

Kahn, Robert L., and Charles F. Cannell. *The Dynamics of Interviewing: Theory, Technique, and Cases.* New York: Wiley, 1957.

Kasper, Gabriele. "Repair in Foreign Language Teaching." *Studies in Second Language Acquisition* 7 (1985): 200–15.

Kramsch, Claire. "Classroom Interaction and Discourse Options." *Studies in Second Language Acquisition* 7 (1985): 169–83.

Lado, Robert. *Language Testing: The Construction and Use of Foreign Language Tests.* New York: McGraw-Hill, 1961.

Lantolf, James P., and William Frawley. "Oral Proficiency Testing: A Critical Analysis." *Modern Language Journal* 69, no. 40 (1985): 337–45.

————. "Proficiency: Understanding the Construct." *Studies in Second Language Acquisition* 10 (1988): 181–95.

Lantolf, James P., and Aneta Pavlenko. "Sociocultural Theory and Second Language Acquisition." *Annual Review of Applied Linguistics* 15 (1995): 108–24.

————, and Gabriela Appel, eds. *Vygotskian Approaches to Second Language Research.* Norwood, N.J.: Ablex, 1998.

Lazaraton, Anne. "The Structural Organization of a Language Interview: Conversation Analytic Perspective." *System* 20 (1992): 373–86.

Levinson, Stephen C. *Pragmatics.* Cambridge: Cambridge University Press, 1983.

Lightbown, Patsy. "Exploring Relationships between Developmental and Instructional Sequences in L2 Acquisition." In *Classroom-Oriented Research in Second Language Acquisition,* edited by Herbert W. Seliger and Michael H. Long, 217–43. Rowley, Mass.: Newbury House, 1983.

Liskin-Gasparro, Judith E. "The ACTFL Proficiency Guidelines: Gateway to Testing and Curriculum." *Foreign Language Annals* 17 (1984): 475–89.

Long, Michael H. "Questions in Foreigner Talk Discourse." *Language Learning* 31 (1981): 135–57.

————. (1983). "Native Speaker and Non-Native Speaker Conversation, and the Negotiation of Comprehensible Input." *Applied Linguistics* 4 (1983): 126–41.

Long, Michael H., and Charlene J. Sato. "Classroom Foreigner Talk Discourse: Forms and Functions of Teachers' Questions." In *Classroom-Oriented Research in Second Language Acquisition*, edited by Herbert W. Selinker and Michael H. Long, 286–85. Rowley, Mass.: Newbury House, 1983.

Lowe, Pardee. "The ILR Interview: Origins, Applications, Pitfalls, and Implications." *Die Unterrichts Praxis* 2 (1983): 230–40.

————. "Proficiency: Panacea, Framework, Process? A Reply to Kramsh, Schultz, and in Particular, to Bachman and Savignon." *Modern Language Journal* 70, no. 4 (1986): 391–96.

————. *ILR Handbook on Oral Interview Testing*. Washington, D.C.: Defense Language Institute/Foreign Service Institute Oral Interview Project, 1988.

Lynch, Brian. *Language Program Evaluation: Theory and Practice*. Melbourne: Cambridge University Press, 1996.

Maccoby, Eleanor E., and Nathan Maccoby. "Interview: A Tool of Social Science." Chapter 12 in *Handbook of Social Psychology*. Vol. 1, *Theory and Method*, ed. Gardner Lindzey. Cambridge, Mass: Addison-Wesley, 1954.

Magnan, Sally Sieloff. "Assessing Speaking Proficiency in the Undergraduate Curriculum: Data from French." *Foreign Language Annals* 19 (1986): 429–38.

McCarthy, Michael. *Discourse Analysis for Language Teachers*. Cambridge: Cambridge University Press, 1991.

McCarthy, Michael, and Ronald Carter. *Language as Discourse: Perspectives for Language Teaching*. London: Longman, 1994.

McHoul, Alexander. "The Organization of Turns at Formal Talk in the Classroom." *Language in Society* 7 (1978): 183–213.

————. "The Organization of Repair in Classroom Talk." *Language in Society* 19 (1990): 349–77.

McNamara, Tim. *Measuring Second Language Performance*. London: Addison Wesley Longman, 1996.

Mehan, Hugh. *Learning Lessons: Social Organization in the Classroom.* Cambridge: Harvard University Press, 1979.

Messick, Samuel. "Validity." In *Educational Measurement,* edited by Robert L. Linn, 13–104. New York: Macmillan, 1989.

Mishler, Elliot. *Research Interviewing: Context and Narrative.* Cambridge: Harvard University Press, 1986.

Moll, Luis C., ed. *Vygotsky and Education: Instructional Implications and Applications of Sociohistorical Psychology.* Cambridge: Cambridge University Press, 1990.

Moskowitz, Gertrude. "The Classroom Interaction of Outstanding Foreign Language Teachers." *Foreign Language Annals* 9 (1976): 135–57.

Moss, Pamela A. "Shifting Conceptions of Validity in Educational Measurement: Implications for Performance Assessment." *Review of Educational Research* 62, no. 3 (Fall 1992): 229–58.

Ochs, Elinor. (1979). "Transcription as Theory." In *Developmental Pragmatics,* edited by Elinor Ochs and Bambi B. Schieffelin, 43–72. New York: Academic Press, 1979.

Oller, John W. "Evidence of General Language Proficiency Factor and Expectancy Grammar." *Die Neueren Sprachen* 76 (1976): 165–74.

———. *Language Tests at School.* London: Longman, 1979.

———, ed. *Issues in Language Testing Research.* Rowley, Mass.: Newbury House, 1983.

Omaggio, Alice. *Teaching Language in Context: Proficiency-Oriented Instruction.* Boston: Heinle and Heinle, 1986.

Osgood, Charles. *The Measurement of Meaning.* Urbana: University of Illinois Press, 1957.

Pica, Teresa P., and Michael H. Long. "The Linguistic and Conversational Performance of Experienced and Inexperienced Teachers." In *Talking to Learn: Conversation in Second Language Acquisition,* edited by Richard R. Day, 85–98. Rowley, Mass.: Newbury House, 1986.

Pomeranz, Anita. "Agreeing and Disagreeing with Assessments: Some Features of Preferred/Dispreferred Turn Shapes." In *Structures of Social Action: Studies in Conversational Analysis,* edited by J. Maxwell and John Heritage, 57–107. The Hague: Mouton, 1984.

Popham, W. James. *Modern Educational Measurement.* Englewood Cliffs: Prentice-Hall, 1981.

Richards, Jack C., and Theodore S. Rodgers. *Approaches and Methods in Language Teaching.* Cambridge: Cambridge University Press, 1986.

Ross, Steven. "Accommodative Questions in Oral Proficiency Interviews." *Language Testing* 9 (1992): 173–86.

Ross, Steven, and Richard Berwick. "The Discourse of Accommodation in Oral Proficiency Examinations." *Studies in Second Language Acquisition* 14 (1992): 159–76.

Sacks, Harvey, Emanuel A. Schegloff, and Gail Jefferson. "A Simplest Systematics for the Organization of Turn Taking in Conversation." *Language* 50, no. 4 (1974): 696–735.

Saussure, Ferdinand de. *Course in General Linguistics.* New York: Philosophical Library, 1959.

Savignon, Sandra J. *Communicative Competence: Theory and Classroom Practice.* Reading, Mass.: Addison-Wesley, 1983.

———. "Evaluation of Communicative Competence: The ACTFL Provisional Proficiency Guidelines." *Modern Language Journal* 69 (1985): 129–33.

Saville-Troike, Muriel. *The Ethnography of Communication.* Oxford: Basil Blackwell, 1982.

Schegloff, Emanuel A., and Harvey Sacks. "Opening up Closings." *Semiotics* 8 (1973): 287–327.

Schegloff, Emanuel A., Gail Jefferson, and Harvey Sacks. "The Preference for Self-Correction in the Organization of Repair in Conversation." *Language* 53 (1977): 361–82.

Schiffrin, Deborah. "Conversational Analysis." *Annual Review of Applied Linguistics* 11 (1990): 3–16.

———. *Discourse Markers.* Cambridge: Cambridge University Press, 1987.

———. *Approaches to Discourse.* Oxford: Blackwell Publishers, 1994.

Searle, John R. *Speech Acts: An Essay in the Philosophy of Language.* Cambridge: Cambridge University Press, 1969.

Shohamy, Elena. "Affective Considerations in Language Testing." *Modern Language Journal* 66 (1982): 13–17.

———. "The Stability of Oral Proficiency Assessment on the Oral Interview Testing Procedures." *Language Learning* 33 (1983): 527–40.

———. "A Proposed Framework for Testing the Oral Language of Second/Foreign Language Learners." *Studies in Second Language Acquisition* 10 (1988): 165–79.

Schinke-Llano, Linda. "On the Value of a Vygotskian Framework for SLA Theory and Research." *Language Learning* 43 (March 1993): 121–29.

Silverman, David. "Interview Talk: Bringing off a Research Instrument." In *Organizational Work: The Language of Grading, the Grading of Language,* edited by David Silverman and Jill Jones, 133–50. London: Collier Macmillan, 1976.

Sinclair, John M., and David Brazil. *Teacher Talk*. Oxford: Oxford University Press, 1982.

Sinclair, John M., and R. Malcolm Coulthard. *Towards an Analysis of Discourse: The English Used by Teachers and Pupils*. London: Oxford University Press, 1975.

Stanfield, Charles W., and Dorry Mann Kenyon. "Research on the Comparability of the Oral Proficiency Interview and the Stimulated Oral Proficiency Interview." *System* 20 (1992): 347–64.

Stubbs, Michael. *Discourse Analysis: The Sociolinguistic Analysis of Natural Language*. Chicago: University of Chicago Press, 1983.

Tannen, Deborah. *Conversational Style: Analyzing Talk Among Friends*. Norwood, N.J.: Ablex, 1984.

———. *Talking Voices: Repetition, Dialogue and Imagery in Conversational Discourse*. Cambridge: Cambridge University Press, 1989.

Thompson, Irene. "A Study of Interrater Reliability of the ACTFL Oral Proficiency Interview in Five European Languages: Data From ESL, French, German, Russian, and Spanish." *Foreign Language Annals* 28, no. 3 (1995): 407–22.

Van Lier, Leo. *The Classroom and the Language Learner*. London: Longman, 1988.

———. "Reeling, Writhing, Drawling, Stretching, and Fainting in Coils: Oral Proficiency Interviews as Conversation." *TESOL Quarterly* 23 (1989): 489–508.

———. *Interaction in the Language Curriculum: Awareness, Autonomy, and Authenticity*. London: Longman, 1996.

Valdman, Albert. "Introduction to the Assessment of Foreign Language Oral Proficiency." *Studies in Second Language Acquisition* 10, no. 2 (1988): 121–28.

Vygotsky, Lev S. *Mind in Society: The Development of Higher Psychological Processes.* Edited by M. Cole, V. John-Steiner, S. Scribner, and E. Souberman. Cambridge: Harvard University Press, 1978.

———. "The Genesis of Higher Mental Functions." In *The Concept of Activity in Soviet Psychology,* edited by James V. Wertsch., 149–88. Armonk, N.Y.: Sharpe, 1981.

Wertsch, James V. *Vygotsky and the Social Formation of Mind.* Cambridge: Harvard University Press, 1985.

———. "The Voice of Rationality in a Sociocultural Approach to Mind." In *Vygotsky and Education: Instructional Implications and Applications of Sociocultural Psychology,* edited by Lois C. Mall, 111–26. Cambridge: Cambridge University Press, 1990.

Widdowson, Henry G. *Teaching Language as Communication.* Oxford: Oxford University Press, 1978.

Wolfson, Nessa. "Speech Events and Natural Speech: Some Implications for Sociolinguistic Methodology." *Language in Society* 5 (1976): 189–209.

Young, Richard. "Conversational Styles in Language Proficiency Interviews." *Language Learning* 45, no. 1 (1995a): 3–42.

———. "Discontinuous Interlanguage Development and its Implications for Oral Proficiency Rating Scales." *Applied Language Learning* 6 (1995b): 13–26.

———. "Sociolinguistic Approaches to SLA." *Annual Review of Applied Linguistics* 19 (1999): 105–31.

Young, Richard, and Michael Milanovic. "Discourse Variation in Oral Proficiency Interviews." *Studies in Second Language Acquisition* 14 (1992): 440–24.

# Index